DAMNED IF I DO

DAMNED IF I DO

PHILIP NITSCHKE
WITH PETER CORRIS

MELBOURNE
UNIVERSITY
PRESS

MELBOURNE UNIVERSITY PUBLISHING
An imprint of Melbourne University Publishing Limited
11–15 Argyle Place South, Carlton, Victoria 3053, Australia
mup-info@unimelb.edu.au
www.mup.com.au

First published 2013
Text © Philip Nitschke and Peter Corris, 2013
Design and typography © Melbourne University Publishing Limited, 2013

Cover design by Philip Campbell Design
Typeset by TypeSkill
Printed in Australia by McPherson's Printing Group

National Library of Australia Cataloguing-in-Publication entry
Nitschke, Philip Haig, author.
Damned if I do/Philip Nitschke with Peter Corris.

9780522861419 (paperback)
9780522861426 (ebook)

Nitschke, Philip Haig.
Physicians—Australia—Biography.
Social reformers—Australia—Biography.
Euthanasia—Australia.
Right to die—Australia.

Other Authors/Contributors:
Corris, Peter, 1942– author.

610.92

For Fiona

You're the starch in my collar
You're the lace in my shoe
You will always be my necessity
I'd be lost without you.

'You're the Cream in My Coffee'
B.G. DeSylva, Lew Brown and Ray Henderson

CONTENTS

From this distant vantage point, the Earth might not seem of any particular interest. But for us, it's different. Look again at that dot. That's here. That's home. That's us. On it everyone you love, everyone you know, everyone you ever heard of, every human being who ever was, lived out their lives. The aggregate of our joy and suffering, thousands of confident religions, ideologies, and economic doctrines, every hunter and forager, every hero and coward, every creator and destroyer of civilization, every king and peasant, every young couple in love, every mother and father, hopeful child, inventor and explorer, every teacher of morals, every corrupt politician, every 'superstar', every 'supreme leader', every saint and sinner in the history of our species lived there—on a mote of dust suspended in a sunbeam.

The earth from 6 billion kilometres

Carl Sagan, *Pale Blue Dot: A Vision of the Human Future in Space*, 1994

PART I

ONE

A good idea

euthanasia *n. 1. painless death. 2. the putting to death of a person painlessly.*

Macquarie Dictionary

I'd rented a shed in Palmerston, a satellite suburb of Darwin, and set it up as a makeshift office for my after-hours practice. I would head off for work at about sunset and go through until midnight or later, and then come back to sleep at the office. This was in the Dry, as I recall, but it's hot all the year round in Darwin; a sheet was all the covering you needed.

I woke up in the shed at about nine o'clock one morning in early 1995 and switched on the radio. Marshall Perron, Chief Minister of the Northern Territory and a member of the conservative Country Liberal Party from 1974 until his retirement from politics later in 1995, was on the ABC news. He spoke about his government's intention to introduce a Bill to legislate for terminally ill people to have the right to get medical help to die at the time of their choosing. This was the first—and only—time I'd ever found myself in agreement with the man and his politics. I thought: *That makes sense*, and went back to sleep.

So there was no 'road to Damascus moment' that transformed my thinking. I simply thought that if I were terminally ill, I'd want to be able to end it when I chose. Common sense. The fact was I'd never given euthanasia a serious thought. The 'e' word had never been mentioned at Sydney University Medical School. The nearest we'd come to it were some final-year lectures on palliative care by an associate professor called Norelle Lickiss, whose religious principles were all too obvious.[1]

Later that day, I was surprised to hear a statement by Dr Chris Wake, President of the Northern Territory branch of the Australian Medical Association (AMA), denouncing the proposal as 'irresponsible', and saying no doctor in the Territory would have a bar of it.

People have different views and that's fine with me, but it was the arrogance of the declaration that no doctor would support the legislation that got my attention. Why the vehemence? Why the implication that any doctor who favoured the proposal was beyond the pale?

As I went about my practice, I spoke to a few people about the matter and found that, almost without exception, their opinion was that terminally ill people should have the sort of rights Perron was advocating. So I had two strands of thought. What about the patients: had anyone asked them for their views? And what right did the AMA have to speak for all doctors in the Northern Territory?

Having always been interested in the intersection between politics and medicine, I decided to find out how the land lay with other members of the profession. I was quite sure that Wake wouldn't have had bothered to have a thorough look at doctors' attitudes.

I spoke to doctors in person and on the phone, and gathered the signatures of twenty-two Territory doctors who supported the legislation. On 8 May 1995 we ran a half-page advertisement in the *NT News*, calling ourselves 'Doctors for Change'.

A public claim has been made that the medical practitioners in the Northern Territory are opposed to the introduction of the Private Member's Bill on the rights of the terminally ill.

This is not the case.

The undersigned doctors are registered practitioners within the Northern Territory and are of the opinion that with the provision of safeguards, voluntary euthanasia should be available to all those terminally ill patients who make such a request.

There is a need for legislation to govern this practice and we support in principle the proposed Bill.

A few weeks later, I sat in the public gallery in the Territory Parliament, listening to the debate on Perron's Bill. There was a lot of public reaction to the newspaper advertisement. It was now clear that there were doctors in the Territory who supported the legislation, and, as the initiator of the ad I found I'd fallen into the role of spokesman for voluntary euthanasia. When they wanted a statement supporting the Bill, the media began coming to me. Wake had been busy campaigning against the Bill, conducting surveys and making statements. He'd even tried to run the line that the Bill was racist, that it was directed against Aboriginal people, a version of the 'poison waterhole' tactic in frontier days (the practice of poisoning the enemy's sources of fresh water) that has come to represent a method of genocide for Aboriginal people. This didn't convince anyone, including the Indigenous people, but it did some damage, and support on the political left faded.

The falling away of support was largely the fault of Perron. As leader of a redneck, conservative government he often railed against socially progressive issues.[2] Understandably, many on the left—unionists and student groups—criticised the Bill as a way of taking a swipe at Perron, without considering the bigger issue.

And it was never going to be hard for opponents to get Aboriginal groups to complain that they hadn't been consulted, because it was true; Perron should have covered that base. It was all too easy to claim that Aboriginal people would stay away from health clinics if they thought euthanasia was part of this government's agenda. I heard these arguments being wheeled out against the Bill as the sitting dragged on. I'd already rescheduled some visits to patients to allow me to hear the debate, but I became increasingly convinced that the Bill would fail, so I left Parliament to start my nightly rounds. In between visits, I was stunned to hear on the radio that the Bill had passed, on the casting vote of the only Aboriginal member, Wes Lanhupuy.

With the Act not due to be implemented until 1 July the following year, I got on with my life, going bush whenever I could and standing as a Senate candidate for the Greens in the 1995 federal election. The Greens were just finding their feet and had approached me as someone to wave a progressive flag. As a person with a track record of opposition to nuclear ships, foreign military bases and uranium mining, I more or less fitted their profile. During that initial campaign I learned how difficult it can be to get a message across at election time. This insight would serve me well when I had a few more forays into politics later on.

It would be a full thirteen months before the *Rights of the Terminally Ill (ROTI) Act* would come into force. In retrospect, its provisions, in terms of the necessary age, medical and mental condition of the patient and the number and status of doctors needed to sign off on the euthanasia procedure, were very conservative. Nevertheless, it was the first piece of legislation of its kind in the world and this struck me forcibly, as did my responsibility. When I saw the world's media, replete with satellite dishes, set up outside Darwin's Parliament House on 1 July 1996 I was shocked, and realised the importance of this new law.

With the hindsight of my knowledge of how things have worked out in other parts of the world, I can see that the

Northern Territory, for all its basic conservatism, and even though it was a close-run thing, had the right conditions to get the law passed. The personality and political power of Marshall Perron were critical. He was a local (and actually born in Darwin), was sufficiently charismatic and knew his electorate intimately. When he let it be known he was intending to retire, his supporters, I think, backed the ROTI Act almost as a reward, indeed a going-away present, for his service.

Second, the Northern Territory has no upper house, which makes passing legislation, especially progressive legislation, easier, given that upper houses are notoriously conservative. The Territory is also the least religious part of Australia, which helped to reduce one source of opposition. Finally, there is something about the mindset of the place that worked in favour of the change. Territory cars carry such numberplates as 'Frontier Australia', 'Barra Country' and 'Outback', which are symbolic of history and myth. Many Territorians see themselves as rugged in comparison with the effete south. In some ways, I believe, the Territory welcomed the voluntary euthanasia legislation precisely because no other state or territory had the guts to deal with this political hand grenade.

This attitude reminded me of when, to earn some money as a PhD student, I was marking final-year matriculation examination papers in physics. (At that time, South Australia administered these exams for the Territory.) One question was unusual: estimate the weight of a brick house. After nearly two weeks of marking the answers from South Australian students, a final, rather grubby, batch of papers arrived from the Territory. In the first answer I read, the student had written something like, 'Who gives a shit we don't have bricks up here.' I had to give him or her a zero, but I felt a grudging respect for that kind of attitude, and still do.

TWO

Country boy

I never got to know my many relations that live all over the Adelaide hills.

Philip Nitschke, 2011

There are lots of Nitschkes in South Australia, all descendants it seems of the same family who arrived, in 1839, on a ship called the *Zebra* captained by Dirk Hahn. They were Lutherans, escaping persecution in Germany, where the Catholic church still held sway. My great-great-grand father was Friedrich William Nitschke, who came to South Australia with his wife and three sons. He was a skilled man, a mason. One of the other heads of the family was a wheelwright and others were described as 'cottagers', meaning small-scale farmers.

Farming was the occupation most of these German immigrants followed for several generations, primarily in the Adelaide Hills and the Barossa Valley, and mainly they moderately prospered. My father, Harold, broke the mould. The family farm was a going concern—mixed farming, animals and crops—but he was one of the younger brothers in a big brood and there was no place for him on the farm or on the land, so he became a primary-school teacher, working mainly in small country towns.

I was born on 8 August 1947 in just such a town, Ardrossan, which was named after a place in Scotland. Ardrossan is on the east coast of the Yorke Peninsula, about 150 kilometres from Adelaide. I have a brother, Dennis, and a sister, Gailene, both older than me.

Looking back, I can see that my father wasn't the farming type anyway. He loved country life but was keen on motor-bikes, home crafts of various kinds and the hunting (for hides) that went along with that. He tanned skins and made things out of leather—a sideline that made him some money. We were never close. In those days, it was common for there to be emotional distance between fathers and sons, and our relationship was like that. I found him difficult, but at times of crisis, and there were a few in my young life, he was always supportive.

My mother, Gwen, is a different story. She's of English and Irish stock, and her maiden name was Richardson. She was brought up on a farm near Penong, which was a small place on the edge of the Nullarbor, about as far west as you can get in South Australia. That's marginal country and the farm was pretty much a subsistence operation. She hated country life with all its restricted opportunities—she had no secondary education, presumably because of distance, and lack of money and encouragement. Her older sister Connie had been sent to Adelaide for further schooling at Presbyterian Ladies College, but hard times meant this was not on offer for Gwen. The family had some bad luck as well; there were three girls and one boy, Doug. When he was quite young, he was washed off rocks while he was fishing and drowned: the uncle I never knew.

In about 1936 my father was posted to Penong as a teacher, and met my mother when she was sixteen and des-perate to get away. I'm not sure about the nature of their attraction to each other. She's said that 'he was a bit of all right', and old photos show her as a very glamorous young woman. My father might also have represented a ticket out of country life, and so they married. He did take her to Adelaide, which, from her perspective, was the bright lights, but did not do so permanently. He only felt at home in the bush and was happy to be sent from one country town to another by the Education Department.

Remarkably, given her lack of formal education, my mother also became a teacher, learning on the job. She was classified as a TUA, or 'temporary untrained assistant', and she and my father were able to take on two-teacher posts. Much as she disliked the bush and its tiny schools, I suspect she did a better job than a lot of the college-trained teachers. It was a different world, and people, and even education departments, made do with what they had.

Time, and the differences in their temperaments and interests, eroded my parents' relationship. In various ways, my mother let my father know of her disappointment in him. In particular, she had no enthusiasm for his family, whom she found rather boorish. There might have been a touch of anti-German feeling in her attitude, with the two world wars fresh in people's memories, although she'd probably deny it. Anyway, as a consequence we did not have much contact with the German side and I know very little about the Nitschke clan. We saw much more of my mother's people, particularly at Christmas and in summer holidays at Victor Harbor and Murray Bridge. There was a tension between my parents that made for an uncomfortable family life at times— there was never neglect, but it was not exactly a happy family picture either. Eventually, after the Whitlam government passed the 'no fault' legislation, my parents divorced. I was an adult by then.

So we shifted around continually, my older brother and sister and me. Because both our parents were teaching and childcare didn't exist, I was sent to school at age four. This was in 1951, in a little place called Frances, 300 kilometres southeast of Adelaide. I coped, but have faint memories of being teased by the other kids—particularly by girls— for being younger and smaller. The only other memory of Frances I have is of the board that had the school name on it being shot up and splintered one night. Country life.

I don't know how many primary schools I was plucked out of to be deposited in another, often mid-term, but it was quite a few. I had to make new friends and deal with the new arrangements. I know that I went to five different secondary schools. I didn't lose ground educationally, which is a bit surprising. I suppose I learned to be adaptable, to accept being on the move, and that's stayed with me. Nowadays, I don't like living out of a suitcase any more than other people do, but at times it's a necessity.

So I grew up as a real country boy and a fairly happy one. I have only the faintest memory of Ardrossan, and I have to admit that it might be affected by an old photograph of me standing in a wheat field: I ran off to play, or perhaps hide, in the field and got lost, to be eventually found and saved by the family cat. There were family stories about it. But the continual change made it an unusual upbringing. I was encouraged, particularly by my mother, to perform well at school and for some reason I developed a growing interest in the physical world—in how and why things work.

I just loved chemistry. At secondary school in a country town, there weren't many others interested in science; everyone else was interested in playing football and cricket. My bat and ball skills were poor. I was good at gymnastics and okay at swimming but not much else. I spent a lot of time reading magazines like *Popular Mechanics* and getting quite interested in the whole idea of what you could do with chemicals. I read in a school textbook about the basis of explosives and I started to try to make gunpowder—that was quite a challenge in country South Australia. I had to get potassium nitrate, the active ingredient in gunpowder. A chemist in Clare, the nearest significant town, told me that sodium nitrate, also known as saltpetre and used in preserving meat, would do. In our town, Koolunga, there was only one shop, but they had bags of this stuff, for people who wanted to cure their own meat. I bought a lot of it, got some sulphur and crushed-up charcoal, and made gunpowder.

Then I began building little cannons and working out some way of firing the gunpowder using electrical detonation. My best friend at the time was Phillip Lange, who grew up on a farm and spent most of his time playing sport, but was quite intrigued by the idea of manufacturing explosives. We built a small bomb and put it under the water in the local creek, the Broughton River. We'd rigged up the electrical detonation and, when we pressed the plunger we'd made, it blew up impressively underwater. We thought that was fantastic.

Then I became even more ambitious. I started to read and think about more sophisticated explosives, like nitroglycerine, and thought if I could just make this, that would have an impact. I had become a trusted member of the science class at school, as one of the few people interested in chemistry. Tom Bowden was the science master there and he used to give me free rein of the laboratory, in return for helping out and cleaning up. Although I did pay my dues. I remember one time when the class was doing an experiment to demonstrate the enzymatic dissolving of starch with saliva, Bowden said to me, 'You're the science monitor, you can collect the class sample.' So, with my beaker, I had to go around to all the students asking them to spit into it, and, of course, two or three of those bastards deliberately spat onto my hand.

'Oh, sorry.'

But, as I say, I was trusted, and I got access to the chemicals and was allowed to take the odd thing home, including the necessary nitric acid. I had a little laboratory set up in the back yard and was sitting there, gingerly pouring my nitric acid into the glycerine. When I look back at it … well, people lose their hands and their heads. It's dangerous stuff, and my experiments with it didn't work, but I was lucky I didn't lose a limb, or worse.

My parents were vaguely aware of my experiments but not too concerned about them. They thought it was very good that I was taking an interest in these kinds of academic pursuits. My father became annoyed once, though, when I fired one of the cannons I'd made. There was a large explosion and it shot a steel projectile—a bolt about half an inch in diameter—straight through the wall of his galvanised iron shed and out the other side.

Related to this kind of mischief was an incident that got me the only caning I ever received at school. I was having a conflict with another person: my friend Phillip Lange. We'd built these home-made pistols that fired starting-pistol caps. Philip was annoying me, so I took his poetry book out of his locker and fired the pistol straight at it. The cover and the first ten pages disintegrated, and quite a bit of smoke and a stench came out of the locker room.

It was reported to the headmaster, Mr Slee, and Lange and I, and another bloke who just happened to be there, were hauled up before the head to explain. I was the guilty one but the other two wouldn't dob me in. Slee said, 'You're all going to get caned', and we did. I was the bus prefect, with the job of getting everyone into the vehicle for the 18-kilometre trip from Koolunga to the school at Brinkworth, and everyone was impressed by the livid welts I had for the next day or two, and my hand swelled up quite badly.

Then we all got mad keen on model aeroplanes with small internal combustion motors, and Slee, probably trying to steer me towards more peaceful pursuits, gave me a plane of his that had a solid main wing, in contrast to the hollow tissue and balsa ones we were building. It had a big, by our standards, engine: a 5.0-cubic-centimetre glow-plug motor. We spent a lot of time—Lange, me and a couple of others—playing around with model aeroplanes. We were building them and flying them, and using those motors for other things, such as putting them in boats that we raced up and down in the waterholes in the Broughton.

My father and my brother hunted—kangaroos—with .303 rifles. Sensibly, my father forbade me to have a rifle until I was well into my high-school years. In fact, I got into trouble for stealing his .303 and firing it into a tree when I was eleven or twelve. Eventually I saved enough money from part-time jobs to buy a .22 rifle. With this I hunted rabbits and foxes. I also had a hunting knife. Questionable now, I know, but I've been around firearms all my life. A knife and a gun were to play unusual roles in my life.

It wasn't all explosions and engines. For instance, I saw a unicyclist at a circus and thought, *I'd like to do that.* I built a unicycle out of spare parts and set about learning to ride it, which I became able to do quite well. It cost me skin and gave me bruises, and it took persistence, but that's an attribute I have.

Religion played no role in my family's life. I was dragged off to church when we visited the Richardsons at Christmas but it made so little impact on me I don't even remember its denomination, though it was probably C of E. I was more exposed to religion in the later stages of my secondary schooling. My mother wanted me to go to university and I'd need solid school results to make it. And as my school at the time, Brinkworth Area School, only went as far as third-year high school, my father decided I should go to Concordia College, a private Lutheran boarding school in Adelaide, which my older brother had also attended.

One snag was that it was an intensely religious institution, and it insisted that all students be confirmed in the Lutheran religion. Somehow, my father knew that an unconfirmed student would certainly receive a large dose of prayer and scripture, something he also knew I wouldn't take kindly to, so he arranged for me to get some instruction in Lutheranism in the local Brinkworth church. This instruction was minimal and uninteresting, but it enabled me to present at the school with my shonky certificate attesting I was a confirmed Lutheran. When I saw the drills the unconfirmed students were subjected to, I was grateful for my father's foresight.

Nevertheless, I was herded with the other boys into chapel every morning. There were prayers at night and on Sundays, with two long church services that were torture. The school aimed to train boys for the ministry, and stressed scripture and Greek and Latin, none of which appealed to me. I wanted to do science, which wasn't held in high esteem, and may even have been viewed with suspicion. I found the school's atmosphere and culture stifling, and begged my parents to put me back in the state system.

I did my final school year at Henley High in Adelaide. That suited me much better but I ran into serious trouble. I was fourteen, not turning fifteen until the August of that year, and 100 kilometres from home—pretty young to be boarding in a strange place with people I didn't know. Not to mince matters, the man in whose house I was boarding was feeling me up whenever he got the chance. This was done in the guise of getting close to me and helping me with my schoolwork—but it was help I didn't need.

You hear a lot about this kind of sexual harassment now, but it was an undiscussed subject back then. Like many people who've had this experience, I didn't know what to do and was frightened. I felt trapped. I'd argued so strongly with my parents to get me out of the Lutheran boarding school and I'd thought the new situation was going to be great, only to find it was worse. As a way of escaping from an intolerable situation, of making a cry for help that couldn't be ignored, I killed the family's pet with my hunting knife.

In any event, I was lucky and unlucky. Lucky, in that my father realised quickly that using a knife to kill a pet dog was unacceptable and dangerous and took me to a psychiatrist to have me psychologically assessed. He knew I would then have a better chance of escaping any kind of juvenile criminal penalty, which is exactly what happened. I was unlucky, in that *The Advertiser* picked up the story. As something indelibly on the public record, this story has been used ever since by those opposed to my work as a campaigner for voluntary euthanasia.

It isn't argument, it's mud-slinging, but it can be effective. Related to this are the slurs that have been levelled at me because of my name: so German-sounding, so like that of the philosopher Nietzsche, so suggestive of Nazism. I'd have avoided much of this if I'd been a Richardson like my mum.

As a result of starting school early and keeping pace with the older students, I was qualified to enter university when I was not yet sixteen. Under the old South Australian system—modelled, I think, on an aspect of English school arrangements (South Australia being a very Anglophile society then)—you could qualify for university entrance after your fourth year of high school. So I'd made it, made university, on the basis of my year at Concordia, despite my problems with the boarding school. My year at Henley High was the one called 'Leaving Honours' and my earlier results stood, despite the disruption caused by killing the dog.

Quite early in my school career, it was obvious that maths and science subjects were where I performed best. My matriculation results—mostly As and a few more Bs— were good enough to get me a Commonwealth scholarship, which paid the university fees and included a small living allowance.

A little naïve perhaps, but not as green as some of those around me, I prepared for university in January 1964. I'd had to deal with a lot of dislocation and a trauma as I moved through adolescence. And, on the positive side, I'd had my first sexual experience with a girl named Trenna when I was thirteen and still at high school in the country and had, at least technically, lost my virginity. Farm girls knew a lot about sex. I felt I was ready for what university had to offer.

THREE

In Adelaide—stormy weather

*I soon chose to study physics, the subject I was best at.
I did not study hard ...*

Philip Nitschke, 2004

Photographs from the 1960s show me with very long hair and a hippie look, a typical left-leaning university student. In those days, my black beret gave me the highly fashionable Che Guevara look. I was never much of a general reader—images interested me more than the written word. As a kid, I was more likely to read comics than books, apart from ones about science. Just as some people have a knack for languages or music, I have a talent, or a knack, for maths and physics, particularly of the more hands-on, experimental variety.

I passed science exams with ease, which is not to say that I found exams easy. I was always anxious, and those three-hour sit-ins when you have to perform under pressure, and your future depends on your performance, stressed me, causing me sleepless nights.

There were ups and downs in my undergraduate years. I was living away from home most of the time, sharing flats and houses with other students. I had jobs in the holidays, of which more later, and I had a car. I also had a girlfriend named Margaret, who was the sister of a friend from university, and I remember a torrid night at the Murray Bridge drive-in watching Elvis in *Love Me Tender*, when we weren't doing other things.

I'd go back to Murray Bridge every weekend and meet up with Margaret, and we'd go to coffee lounges and spend time in the back seat of the car, parked at her parents' house. We used to write to each other every second day. I was sixteen and she was fourteen, and her parents put a stop to things, saying she was not old enough for such a serious relationship. Suddenly I got a letter from her saying she couldn't have anything more to do with me because her parents said she was too young.

This was in the final term of that first year of university and I was terribly upset. I reacted by piling up all her letters and burning them in the incinerator at the back of the boarding house I was then living in. I threw myself into my studies, which was unusual, and with such enthusiasm that I did very well—I topped the year in mathematics and got distinctions in everything I sat for. Being dumped was part of that—it was the spur.

Then, in the holidays, I started to search furiously for a replacement for Margaret and I went to a dance at Norwood with a couple of friends. I met Jenny there and was completely captivated by her. She was an apprentice hairdresser, and was very fashionably dressed and very beautiful. I'd never met anyone like her. This was not only because she was so good looking but because she was at ease in any company. I was shy—I still am, and have to push myself in social situations. Just being with her boosted my confidence and helped me to cope socially; she was so attractive, and her prestige rubbed off on me. We were together through the holidays and the following year, and stayed together for the best part of a decade.

I was never quite sure what attracted Jenny to me. She was gregarious and adventurous. I'd describe her as someone who would go to the moon, who was ready for anything, so, I suppose, there was a wild streak in me that must have appealed to her, at least for a time.

I attracted the attention of the media again in my second year at university. One night, my precious portable transistor radio was stolen from my car when it was parked outside the St Clair Recreation Centre in Woodville. The thing to do every Saturday night was go there to a dance, to meet people—girls, in particular. I reported the theft to the police, and the officer at the desk—who was quite nice, in fact—told me bluntly that I'd be unlikely to see it again and said there was little the police would be able do about it. I carried on a bit, but he told me to be realistic, that it wasn't the greatest crime in the world.

I was angry and I wasn't accepting that, so I borrowed my father's car and put an imitation radio on its dashboard, leaving the window down slightly. I got my friend Jim Thomson, a fellow physics student, to drive the car to much the same place it had been parked in before. I stayed in the boot with my rifle, while Jim and Jenny went in to the dance. I had the boot not quite closed, so when I heard two people mumbling, and felt the car lurch, I threw open the lid. One ran, but I stuck the rifle in the other one's face and told him he was under a citizen's arrest.

As this was well before mobile phones, I marched him, with his hands up, to the nearest house, knocked on the door and asked the man who answered to ring the police. There was a bit of pandemonium, because it must have looked like a hold-up to him, but he rang the police, and they showed up very quickly.

The guy I'd bailed up said, 'Look, I was just walking down the street and this crazy jumps out of a car, with a gun.'

One of the police said to me, 'What's your side of the story?'

I convinced them that I was telling the truth. They took the bloke across the road to where it was dark, pushed him over roughly, picked him up and then did it again. That was an eye-opener. One of them came back to where I was and told me the guy had confirmed my story.

'By the way,' he said, 'that gun isn't loaded, is it?'

I said it wasn't, but it was. He left and went on with the 'interrogation' over the road, and I was sitting there, getting bullets out of the rifle as fast as I could and spilling them all over the place. The policeman returned, saw what was happening and chose not to notice, but told me I'd come close to being in very serious trouble and never to do anything like that again.

The police went to the suspect's place and found it stacked with stolen goods. I got my transistor back but it never worked as well as it had, and it was covered in Port Adelaide Football Club stickers—and I hated Port Adelaide.

Somehow, word got around about my citizen's arrest and the story appeared on the front page of *The Advertiser*. A television station asked me to give them an interview. I did (my first), and a picture of me holding the gun was shown. I gave them chapter and verse on how the police had said there was nothing they could do. Soon after that, a police inspector came visiting.

'Look,' he said, 'that constable you named on television is now in quite a bit of trouble. We're not supposed to tell the public there's nothing the police can do.'

He produced a statement for me to sign that, in more diplomatic language, had me admitting that what I'd said was bullshit. I remembered the desk constable as being a nice bloke and the inspector spoke well of him, so I thought, *What the hell*, and signed the statement. About two months later, I got a letter from the Commissioner of Police commending me as a model citizen. So for lying I got a commendation. There was a lesson in that: organisations are not always what they seem and don't always do what they say. The two newsworthy events I was involved in also taught me that solving your own problems can cast you as a hero or a villain, depending on the perspective.

The rifle itself was a Browning .22 automatic my father had given me. I liked it—it had an eight-round stock magazine, and broke in the middle and folded down to a very compact size. I waited until the very last day to surrender it under John Howard's gun buyback that was passed after the Port Arthur massacre. I happened to be in Victoria, and Bendigo was the nearest place where guns could be handed in. I had tears in my eyes when I brought it in. I said I was planning to go sailing and it would be a good idea to have a gun. The sergeant said, 'You can have a gun, but you can't have an automatic like this one.' But he took pity on me, saying something like, 'Got sentimental value, has it, son?' I said it had been my father's, and he let me go in to where they had the guillotine, and I watched silently as it destroyed the rifle.

★ ★ ★

I always worked in the holidays. I did fruit picking at the end of my last school year and, after my first year at university, I got a job at the James Hardie factory in Adelaide. I was dealing with tyres but there was the odd brush with asbestos, which I don't like thinking about. The next year I thought, *I'm not going back to that place*, because, god, it was hard work lugging tyres around. So, in 1966, I got a job at the Weapons Research Establishment in Salisbury. It was established, as I understand it, to facilitate the Woomera rocket program, and a lot of the peripheral scientific equipment needed was developed there, so, in the holidays, they were taking on university science students to assist with various projects. The first year I was with an electronic development unit, and things went well; in the second year I got a really interesting project in night vision. They were investigating whether the Australian Army should spend money on purchasing expensive new night-vision glasses that had been developed in America or whether they should just issue everyone with good binoculars. I found myself sitting in a totally dark room for the first three hours of the day, getting dark adapted, and then going into a test tunnel to look at low-illuminated targets at certain distances, and using image intensifiers and binoculars to see how they compared. I enjoyed the work. I had to be careful, though, wearing red goggles so that I didn't lose my dark adaption when I left the tunnel. I'd be sitting in the cafeteria at lunchtime with my bright red goggles on. People found that intriguing.

During my last year of university, I worked at the laboratories of the Highways Department, with one of the pieces of nuclear equipment they'd just acquired. The device emitted radiation when placed on a newly made road, and the reflected signal gave information on the soil density and water content. I liked these holiday jobs; they were interesting and the money helped too.

In the 1960s, as was the case with so many of my generation—the baby boomers—my politics moved steadily to the left. The Vietnam War was raging and I was totally opposed to it. I was just the right age to be balloted in as a conscript, which I wanted no part of. One day I watched sombrely as a gun carriage moved slowly down King William Street in Adelaide. It carried the coffin of Errol Novak, someone I'd known at boarding school, who was the first Australian conscript to be killed in Vietnam. He seemed to have missed out on many of the good things in life. At school he had often been targeted by the gangs that ruled the dormitories, and now here he was, a victim of an unjust war. Friends more courageous than me resisted the draft and spent years in hiding up in Queensland, avoiding the police. To my mind, they were the real heroes. I took the much easier course of joining the University Air Squadron, which gave me exemption in return for minimal military involvement.

These days I watch with growing alarm as society forgets the obscenity that was Vietnam.

Although I was excited by physics and had thoughts of a career in the field, I did regret that I hadn't had wider horizons when I first enrolled at university. One day in first-year science, I persuaded a friend I'd met who was doing medicine to smuggle me into a dissecting session. I was intrigued, fascinated, even. I made enquiries about changing from science to medicine but was told it just wasn't possible. Universities were rigid and inflexible, with strict protocols in place. But, there was a seed planted.

★ ★ ★

My childhood was littered with practical jokes and I kept them up at university. One in particular I remember playing on my friend Theo. For some reason, we had to have annual medical checks at university and you had to provide a urine sample. Theo's appointment was after mine.

He said, 'How much do you have to give?'

I said, 'Oh, I was told what I had wasn't enough and I had to give some more. You need a fair bit, say, a Coke-bottle full.'

He said, 'I can't fill a bloody Coke bottle.'

I told him just to take his time and he'd be all right. He eventually managed to fill the bottle, and took it in while the others were there with little containers discreetly wrapped in tissue. He handed his bottle over and the nurse looked at him as if he were mad. That was pretty funny, so I continued. The following week I told him that there was a message on the noticeboard that everyone had to go back in and get their containers.

'I've come to collect my container,' Theo announced at the desk. The nurse looked at him oddly then went off, returning with a shoe box containing many tiny containers, and the one large Coke bottle. Theo picked up the bottle and left. I have no idea what the nursing staff thought, but I found this very funny and still smile when I think back. My jokes weren't malicious, but you wouldn't want to be on the wrong end of them.

Another memory from undergraduate days is of an experience that, for a short time, shook my atheism. I went into some detail about this in an interview with Scott Stephens for the ABC program *Compass*. He asked me if I believed in God and I said I didn't because, as a physical scientist, I needed evidence to support my beliefs. But I admitted to having moments of questioning whether there might be a god.

The most bizarre of these was the experience that occurred when I was in my undergraduate years at Adelaide University. I woke up one morning and had really swollen feet. I couldn't stand on them; I was in a dreadful state. I couldn't get to university and I was sitting there thinking, *What the hell am I going to do?* Later that morning I opened a Bible that was there in the boarding house and the first words I read were 'King Asa was diseased in his feet, and he cursed God'. And I thought, *How many references to feet are there in the Bible? What is the statistical probability of opening the Bible and reading about feet when you've got a problem with your own?* A miracle, if you like, and I was shaken.

Scott asked me if I'd prayed at that moment and I said that I might have, but the fleeting feeling of the existence of a god faded quickly, and my atheism reasserted itself. I now see the event as just an improbable coincidence. The problem turned out to be a case of chilblains.

★ ★ ★

My undergraduate career at the University of Adelaide ended not with a whimper but with a bang. As a final-year honours project, I aimed to create a hologram. It would be Australia's first. This was ambitious; optics was not a field of physics of particular interest to the Adelaide department, which spe-cialised in other areas like space, atmospheric and solid-state physics. But I was intrigued by the idea of a three-dimensional image, suspended in space, which could be captured in time and frozen as an exposure on a glass photographic plate. There were technical problems, to do with the slowness of the only available high-resolution red-sensitive film, which meant that a three-hour exposure time would be needed in conditions of utter stillness. Any movement of a millionth of a centimetre would destroy the process and you didn't dare breathe while the experiment was running. The only place it could be conducted was in the seismic vault—a chamber built deep in the basement and specially designed for seismological meas-urements. I had permission to use it and the best time to do so was on a Sunday night, when traffic outside was at a minimum.

After a good number of failures I was getting somewhere, but time was running out and the exams were looming. On the last Sunday night that the vault was available to me, I found the door was locked. I was alone and enraged. I was also damned if I was going to let a housekeeping glitch (and it might've been more than that because there were people who weren't happy with this use of the vault) thwart my experiment.

I gave the door a huge frustrated kick and it flew off its hinges. Surprisingly, I didn't hurt my foot and I later reflected that this must be what happens when karate practitioners break bricks with their hand—that if what you strike gives way, you don't feel the pain of the impact.

The experiment was a success—the image was captured and I was briefly the hero of the department. Everybody visited the lab to view the image. There was one anxious moment: someone dropped the glass plate and it broke into many pieces. It didn't matter, though—the full image remained on all the broken pieces, one of the many intrigu-ing aspects of holography.

Star I might have been, but I was summoned to the office of Professor Carver, the head of the department. He was sympathetic but made it clear that there would need to be disciplinary action. I was fined five dollars, to go, the letter said, towards repairing the wilful damage I'd caused to university property. But it was this experiment that probably led to me receiving a first-class honours degree in physics.

With the first in my pocket, I got a very attractive offer from the Boeing Corporation in Seattle to work on acoustic physics and noise abatement, which were areas that interested me. I was very tempted. I was twenty and wanted see the world. However, at the Boeing interview I was alarmed to find that someone of my age coming to the US to work wasn't necessarily exempt from service in the US military. They said they'd secured their employees a lot of exemptions, but they couldn't guarantee it.

This was in 1968, and the Vietnam War was escalating, my opposition to it growing harder by the day as I spent a few months deciding whether or not to take the job. Boeing even sent me a subscription to the *Seattle Times* to help me get a feel for life in the city, but the war news kept getting worse. I was offered a PhD scholarship at Flinders University. Boeing wasn't interested in me obtaining a doctorate, or in holding the job open, so I opted for Flinders.

FOUR

Aiming higher—direction uncertain

Scientists love lasers.

Saul Goodman in *Breaking Bad*

My postgraduate years were not easy, on both the personal and academic fronts, although PhD scholarships were more generous then: if you supplemented your scholarship with a bit of tutoring, you could afford to pay rent and generally have a reasonable standard of living. However, I'd been with Jenny for three years and her parents started pressuring us to get married. Her parents were very protective of her, perhaps because she was adopted.

This was the late 1960s, when single women still had a lot of trouble getting prescriptions for the Pill. Like many at the time, we used pretty unsatisfactory methods of contraception and had quite a few scares. I remember more than one month that seemed to go on forever. I would be throwing up from sheer anxiety until Jenny would finally phone to tell me we were in the clear.

Worrying about an unwanted pregnancy was probably at the heart of her parents' enthusiasm for their daughter to be married. So we went ahead—booked the cars, arranged the reception; our parents met, and all the rest of it. Then I developed blinding headaches. They went on for weeks, while I was trying to make a start on the research for my PhD.

I went to doctor after doctor, had test after test, but no cause was found. Eventually, one of the senior physicians I'd been referred to at Royal Adelaide Hospital, who knew I was about to be married, said he thought the wedding could have something to do with it.

I just looked at him.

'Have you thought about calling it off?'

He wrote me a note; I suppose it was something about me having a nervous condition. Armed with this, I went to Jenny and said I couldn't get married. She took it surprisingly well, then added that she had never particularly wanted to get married anyway.

But when we told her parents they were horrified. Her father actually attacked me physically, throwing punches. I had to fist-fight him off. While this was going on, Jenny's mother fell to the floor.

She screamed, 'I'm having a heart attack, Dick. I'm having a heart attack!'

'Not now, Marj!' he said, shaping up.

It ended with Jenny being locked in her room. Not one to accept this, she threw what she needed into a bag and climbed out of the window. I was still scuffling with Dick when she walked past the window and waved at me to come along. I extracted myself and we took off.

It was sad, really. She was something of an outcast after that and had to get the police to help her recover her belongings from her parents' house. However, we would be together for another five years.

Getting out of the wedding wasn't the end of my medical problems. The doctor who'd put his finger on the cause of the headaches suggested that I have a psychiatric review; hypochondria must have crossed his mind. I did so, reporting that the headaches had gone. The next thing I knew I was in the psychiatric ward of the Royal Adelaide and they were telling me I could benefit from a period of voluntary residential care. Someone was sent to my flat and, in case I was a danger to others, confiscated the guns and knives I used for hunting. This scared the hell out of my flatmate Theo, who wondered what sort of a person he'd been living with.

So there I was, stuck in hospital for two weeks and unable to get on with my floundering PhD work. I didn't think their treatment was doing me any good, so to get myself out I carefully answered all the questions in the next assessment, not honestly, but in a way I felt would convince them of my sanity. It worked. The psychiatrists decided that I'd made a remarkable recovery and I was released. This left me with considerable scepticism about this field of medicine. One that remains with me.

At Flinders I was active in the anti-Vietnam movement but also took an interest in other social issues. I took part in the protests about the Springboks playing in Adelaide, Aboriginal land rights, and was interested in emerging issues of feminism and the rights of gays and lesbians. These were all valid concerns when coming of age as a baby boomer in Adelaide. One Flinders Postgraduate Students' Association (FPSA) lunch remains particularly memorable. The FPSA would hold regular luncheons; the sherry would be flowing and there would always be a guest speaker but the events were generally pretty dull. When it was announced, however, that there would be a scheduled talk by controversial psychology lecturer Dr John Court, who claimed his aversion therapy cured homosexuality, dull things were not.

A small group of us from the physical sciences department walked across past the campus lake to the union building where the lunches were held; I had my prepared questions in hand. On this occasion I'd spent hours poring over the writings of philosopher and sociologist Herbert Marcuse to get precisely the right angle to make Court squirm. We were itching for a fight on this issue. My problem on the day was that by the time question time came around, I'd drunk way too much sherry. I got up to harangue Court and slurred my words, making something of a mockery of my carefully worded question. On seeing my condition, the marshals at the event quickly moved in, with a view to removing me forcibly. As they grabbed me, I reached out for anything at hand, which happened to be the tablecloth. This led to a dramatic overturning of the table, with its cutlery and my comrades' food and drinks. Needless to say, John Court's hour in the spotlight came to a rapid end.

The lunch would later be written up in *Nation Review*. I can't remember who the journalist was but the opening line of the article was as fine prose as you are likely to read. It started: 'When she arrived with two "No More Duncan" badges impaling her nipples it was clear that this was not going to be your average postgraduate students association luncheon …' The journalist was right.

The Duncan badge referred to the 1972 death of academic Dr George Duncan, a Cambridge graduate who had moved to Adelaide. He was an openly gay man and lectured in law part-time at the University of Adelaide. One night, he and another man were thrown into Adelaide's Torrens River near the University footbridge, which at that time was a well-known gay beat. Duncan drowned. It was suspected that the perpetrators were three senior vice-squad police officers. The coroner returned an open finding on 5 July 1972 and the police investigation, which described the murder as a 'high-spirited frolic gone wrong', didn't provide enough evidence to prosecute any of the suspects. Duncan's death became a rallying point for the gay movement in South Australia, especially since his attackers were never brought to justice.

Another memorable moment from my postgraduate days at Flinders involved the playing of one of Hitler's speeches from the Nuremberg Rallies. Along with another postgraduate physics student, I built a massively powerful audio amplifier. By this time I had my own area in the lab, with my own office, and no one really knew when I was in the building. The laboratories at Flinders were located in the southern foothills and looked down over the suburbs of Adelaide.

The night was quiet, still and very hot. We locked ourselves in and switched on the 'No Entry: Laser in Use' warning sign. We positioned the amplifier, put the directional speakers in the window and played Hitler's Nuremberg speeches at an earth-shattering volume. When the university security people eventually worked out where the sound was coming from, they hammered on the door, used their keys to get in and quickly cut the power. With phone calls from across Adelaide to the police, radio stations and the university, and eventually, with letters of protest pouring in from the suburbs, the university went into damage control, simply announcing that the problem had been solved. They then waited as the fuss died down. We were told to report to the department head, lectured, and warned to stay on good behaviour.

Quite recently, I was interested to learn that the speeches contained, among other things, many exhortations to God—which makes the whole incident even more ridiculous. Clearly, at the time I didn't have any idea what Hitler was saying. But it didn't really matter to me, as it wasn't the message I was interested in. Rather, it was the sheer aural power and theatrics of the Nazi rally—the bellowing voices, the applause. We'd been playing around with laser lights and sound, and they just seemed to fit. What we did was not in good taste, insensitive really. But dissent was in the air and we were trying to shake some of Adelaide's conformity and complacency. We had got the recording on loan from the Adelaide ABC. Curiously, we were never asked why we wanted it.

★ ★ ★

My politics (and antics) were a welcome distraction from the trouble I was having with my thesis. As anyone who has been through it will tell you, studying for a doctorate is a stressful and complex business. It's make or break—success is likely to lead to a worthwhile career; failure can greatly restrict employment options. I came close to missing out on getting my PhD, but it wasn't really my fault.

The choice of a topic is crucial in success with a doctorate: it must be of sufficient weight to be likely to yield results that will merit the degree. Also critical is your relationship with your supervisor. My thesis involved the use of high-energy lasers to measure the temperature and density of plasmas (high-temperature ionised gases). Extracting energy from thermonuclear reactions is one of the holy grails of physics. The project had formidable technical problems but it was the personal ones that were really the issue.

I was not long into the project when I had a falling-out with my supervisor. We didn't get on well for some reason and this would be compounded when I found out more about his background. Perhaps because I'd moved around rural South Australia so much, I'd become interested in the vast, little-travelled space to the north—the Northern Territory. In 1970 I came across a book by Eric Baume entitled *Tragedy Track*, which had been published in 1933. It is the story of the hardships experienced by people working on the Tanami goldfield in Central Australia and contained accounts of the last massacre of Aborigines in Australia, known as the Coniston massacre. This was the revenge killing of an estimated 170 people of the Warlpiri, Anmatyerre and Kaytetye tribes, over the death of a white dingo trapper. The turn-off to Coniston is on the Stuart Highway, about 150 kilometres north of Alice Springs. I can't go past it without thinking of the barbaric events that took place there. Extracts from the Royal Commission report into the massacre mentioned the name of the Northern Territory policeman who instigated the massacre. I happened to ask my supervisor about his background and he told me that during the war he'd come down to Adelaide for school from the Territory. His father had been a policeman up there. Same name, same bloke.

It was unreasonable for me to take a set against him on account of his father's actions but this knowledge didn't help what was an already rocky relationship. I mentioned who his father was to someone; this got back to my supervisor and it was all downhill from then on. He hadn't been much help with the tricky project before, but now he became almost obstructionist, and I was in trouble. As well, he didn't have a good track record for his students getting PhDs.

What usually happened when things went sour with a doctoral candidate's thesis was that he or she was awarded a Masters degree as a consolation prize, which usually meant goodbye to an academic career. I was saved from this fate, first by Mal Phillips, a visiting Canadian lecturer, who more or less took me and the project under his wing. (I was pleasantly surprised when Mal turned up at one of my voluntary euthanasia workshops in Vancouver in 2010.) My second saviour was Max Brennan, head of the department. Professor Brennan couldn't become my official supervisor, as that would have been too much of a slight to my appointed supervisor, but he took over the steering of the research and had a hand in the appointment of my examiners.

But having the PhD didn't smooth my path to an academic career. The Vietnam War may have been winding down but the Cold War was still going on, and those of us on the left were still highly critical of American policies. I learned that Flinders University, along with others in Australia, was accepting funding that could be sourced back to American companies involved in the development of high-tech US weapons.

The thought of my research being even partly funded in this way upset me. Instead of making my protest through university channels—submissions to committees, approaches to faculty deans and the vice-chancellor, etc.—I went public.

My denunciation of the university policy was published in *The Advertiser* and picked up by the ABC. I was interviewed on ABC radio's *AM* program, voicing my anger. Although my demeanour is usually quiet, I can become heated and was on this occasion. Despite his support for me during my earlier difficulties, Professor Brennan was unimpressed. He hauled me in to explain myself. The message, which I received loud and clear, was that what I had done wasn't a good career-in-physics move.

To tell the truth, I wasn't that surprised. In any case, I'd taken longer, owing to the difficulties, with the PhD course than was usual and I felt I'd spent too much time as a student. Other people in the last stages of their PhDs were applying here, there and everywhere for post-docs and anxiously watching for the mail, with commiserations for knock-backs, and celebrations and big piss-ups for successes.

After *AM* though, I received two unexpected letters. One was from the American actor and stage director Hayes Gordon, of the Ensemble Theatre in Sydney, saying something like, 'You've got a future on the stage, boy. Do you want to come and work for me?' The other had been written on a typewriter with missing keys, and read: 'I heard you on *AM*, great stuff. Come and work here, we need people like you.' It was signed Don McLeod. And I'm thinking, *Who the hell's Don McLeod? He can't even type.*

I was about to throw the letter out when I mentioned it to Chris Starr, one of my friends from the politics department. He said, 'Bloody hell, you got a letter from Don McLeod. That's amazing.' The next thing, the letter was doing the rounds of the university and I quickly came up to speed on just who Don McLeod was. I learned that he'd led the first Aboriginal strike in the Pilbara in 1948, the year after I was born, and had written the book *How the West was Lost* about it. There'd been a film about him and he was a legend. He was living on Strelley station, which Indigenous people had bought, and was helping them run it.

Two amazingly different job offers but I didn't take either. I occasionally speculate on just how different life might have been if I had.

FIVE

Wave Hill

It was a rusty little humpy, not more than four feet high, eight feet deep, by perhaps five feet wide. Vincent Lingiari, the elder of the tribe, the sacred Kadijeri man and a noble human being, had had to crawl into this dwelling, often after working from daylight to dark.

Frank Hardy, *The Unlucky Australians*

Don Atkinson was the laboratory and workshops manager at Flinders. I needed materials like glassware and electronics, and mechanical equipment for my project, and so I was dealing with Don all the time, negotiating with him about what I could and couldn't have. He had a strong left-wing political background, which spilled over into all aspects of his life. He was an intriguing person and I got to like him a lot. I was incredibly sad when he died of mesothelioma, in April 2007 and was very glad I had had the chance to talk to him in Adelaide shortly before he died.

He had a little entourage of postgraduate students, all politically left, and we had drinking sessions on Fridays at the Tonsley Park or Flagstaff hotels. We thought ourselves smarter than anyone else—that we knew what was going on. Elitist, really. Don used to go to places like Nigeria, and come back with stories about how things were in the third world and in South Africa. That was inspirational, but he also used to make the point that it was way too easy to carry on about problems overseas; it wasn't that we shouldn't be concerned about them, but that there were things that were very wrong in Australia. Don was the one who first told me about Wave Hill.

The August 1966 strike by Aboriginal stockmen at Wave Hill cattle station in the Northern Territory made news around the world and highlighted Australia's shameful treatment of its Indigenous people. The strike, and the accompanying land rights claim by the Gurindji tribe, led to a struggle that lasted for eight years. The story of those hard years is encapsulated in Frank Hardy's *The Unlucky Australians*, and Kev Carmody and Paul Kelly's well-known song 'From Little Things Big Things Grow'.

A number of Aboriginal leaders toured Australia, seeking political, financial and moral support. In 1971 I attended such a talk at Flinders University given by Lupna Giari, or Captain Major as he was known, one of the Gurindji elders. The strike had gripped my imagination from the start and Lupna's talk intensified my interest. Disenchanted with academic pursuits and with an emerging interest in issues of social justice, I wanted to join in the struggle.

After the talk, I asked Captain Major how I could help and was told a gardener was desperately needed. Over the next weeks, some politicking went on and there was a coup within the post-graduate student association that led to them setting up a fund to pay for a gardener at Wave Hill. This money initially funded my role, although there was other support as well. I wasn't alone in my passionate support for the Gurindji; far from it. Many unions, such as the Waterside Workers Federation, were on side and Frank Hardy's book greatly helped get people interested in this Aboriginal cause.

My intentions were more modest: I wasn't looking to write anything; I just wanted to be of practical help. My initial plan was to go, as a gardener, to where the Gurindji were camped, on strike and hoping for land to run their own cattle station. This was at Daguragu—whitefella name Wattie Creek—around 800 kilometres south-west of Darwin. I knew almost nothing about gardening and wasn't much interested in it, but I was prepared to give it a go, just to be able to help.

However, there was a delay before Jenny and I could leave for Wave Hill. I'd become friendly with Professor Peter Schwerdtfeger in the Department of Oceanography. The department, later renamed Earth Sciences, looked at oceanography, seismology and meteorology. It was running a couple of field stations and one of them was at Cape Du Couedic, the bleak exposed south-west tip of Kangaroo Island. Schwerdtfeger said to me that I looked like someone who needed a break. Presumably, he thought that if I had a rest I might settle down and stop doing self-destructive things like drinking too much and shooting my mouth off!

The oceanography department wanted someone to look after the field station and the lighthouse, and it sounded good to me. There were three houses down at the end of the island, built at the turn of the century for a time when the light had to be tended; now they were deserted and the place was very isolated. I was told that there'd been difficulties with people in the past. Recently, a couple, an ex-laboratory assistant and his partner, had come to grief. She was pregnant, which didn't help, and they had brought a cat, which was forbidden, because the field station land was excised out of the Flinders Chase National Park. The ranger, George Lonzer, kicked them off the island.

Schwerdtfeger said, 'See if you can straighten this mess out. Go down there and write a book or something.' He took Jenny and me out to dinner and painted a picture of the beautiful, peaceful life we could have. So we packed up about ten tea chests of stuff, god knows why, and loaded all on the Troubridge ferry from Port Adelaide. There was a big send-off, as though we were going to London, even though it was only about five hours to the island.

The job paid $11 a week all up to look after the field station, which meant just being there and taking phone calls, and organising for when the oceanographers came over for various research projects. I had to do the meteorology readings at nine and three o'clock and send through the results. It was a spectacular place, but bleak and lonely. In winter, the storms would come in straight off the Southern Ocean and blow hard. Of the three houses two were derelict. Jenny and I got busy fixing up the habitable house, which had National Trust protection and was well fitted out.

There was a deep pool at the bottom of a high, steep cliff, and the previous occupants had left a series of ropes and ladders that enabled a fairly perilous descent. I got a cray pot and every morning would clamber down these ropes and ladders, then get into my wetsuit and swim out. The water was cold but beautifully clear and deep, and I could see my cray pot metres below. I'd pull it up, swim back, pull it ashore, put these giant crays in my rucksack and clamber back up. It was hard work getting the crays, and I sometimes thought I'd eventually lose interest and never eat another crayfish in my life. We were having crayfish morning and night; I'd never eaten much before because of the expense. But it was the ritual that was satisfying—boiling up the copper and dropping in the crays (which did upset me). I also did a lot of spear fishing; we were living off the sea.

An article with a photograph of Jenny and me on the island appeared in the magazine section of Adelaide's *Sunday Mail*, in the wake of the *AM* interview. The headline was 'Heaven and $10'.

After nearly six months, things started to go wrong. We initially had a lot of visitors; we'd do the entertaining, drive them around, take them spear fishing, and they'd say how fantastic everything was. But then we'd drive them to the airstrip at Kingscote and they'd fly back to Adelaide, leaving

Jenny and me alone. There started to be silences between us and weren't getting on well together.

Jenny began baking cakes and selling them to the tourists who came by. But I realised that I was just marking time and had to do something meaningful. Don Atkinson rang up from time to time, and eventually came over to the island. He said, 'Are you serious about going to Wave Hill, or are you just fucking around?'

So it was time to make my apologies to Don McLeod and Hayes Gordon and go. Jenny was up for it. I had a Toyota Land Cruiser FJ40 that I'd bought second-hand, one of the first of that model in Australia, and I spent some time getting it into condition for the trip north. We loaded it up with seeds and gardening tools and set off, like some modern day Johnny Appleseed. The trip was like going up the river in Joseph Conrad's *Heart of Darkness*. The differential broke down in Alice and I had to dismantle it in the Todd riverbed, but it was the hostility from some of the people along the way that shocked us. We had to get rid of the Toyota's stickers protesting against the US Pine Gap base and cope with being called 'southern shit-stirrers'.

On arrival at Wattie Creek, things got off to a bad start. I met David Quinn, who'd been there for a couple of years as a sort of manager of the station's business—writing and answering letters, ordering and paying for things and so on. He was the only literate white male before I arrived, which made him important. I sensed his hostility immediately and later came to understand it. There was also one white woman in the camp named Lynn Raper. She was an amateur linguist who spent most of her time with the women, writing down the language. It was immediately clear that she and David Quinn were in a relationship.

Jenny and I were assigned the saddle shed to put our swag in and it was about a hundred metres from the centre of the camp. Nothing much happened for the first few days, but in the early morning of the fifth day I saw a lot of unusual activity going on. David Quinn was loading his and Lynn's stuff into his old Land Rover. One of the elders, Pincher Numiari, came over to me and said there'd been a lot of trouble in the night. He told me it was going to get nasty, that the police would be involved and I'd best keep right out of it. That's what we did and watched as there was a lot of coming and going; no police, but there were meetings of the elders and a feeling of tension. Neither David Quinn nor Lynn Raper said a word to me. They just drove off in the loaded-up Land Rover.

Shortly after that, Pincher came over and told me that Vincent Lingiari wanted to see me. Vincent was the leader of the Gurindji people, the one who led the Wave Hill Walk Off in 1966. Labor Prime Minister Gough Whitlam would later pour sand into Vincent's hand when the land in question was handed back to the Gurindji. The federal electorate of Lingiari is named in his honour.

I went to where the elders were having their meeting, and no one said anything about what had actually happened between Mike, Lyn and the community, but it was clearly serious enough for the couple to pack up and leave. Vincent just asked me if I wanted to do the job David Quinn had been doing. I said yes. The job of helping run the place had much more appeal than being a gardener. Still, I had mixed emotions. I was excited by the prospect of the more interesting job and pleased that the people seemed to have faith in me, but the tension of the last few days had been high and Jenny and I decided we needed a break. We got in the Toyota and headed off for the closest pub, in Top Springs, 170 kilometres away, for a drink. We hadn't had a drink in a week.

We got to the pub, and there was Quinn's Land Rover. We went into the bar, and I greeted David and Lynn politely.

'What the fuck d'you think you're doing here?' Quinn said.

'Just having a drink.'

'You think you know everything,' he said. 'But you know fucking nothing. You'll never be able to work here.'

Somehow he'd got the idea that I'd been after his job from the start, which wasn't true. He went on about what had happened at the camp. I was angry by this time and responded, criticising him for talking in public about it. It was just a throwaway line but it was the wrong one at the wrong time.

Lynn was there and screamed at David to kill me. We went outside. David was a bit reluctant but shaped up for a fist fight. In the end it came down to pushing and shoving each other, and then he broke away.

'You're not worth it,' he said. He grabbed Lynn's arm and they drove off.

I was sitting on the ground by this time and was a bit shaken. I can understand Lynn's anger. At the very least, she'd received some bad treatment. I later came, like David Quinn, to resent interlopers. This event was a lesson for me in the kinds of tensions that often develop in places like Wave Hill.

Jenny and I were in at the deep end, the only literate people there. I took on the job of being the community's administrative manager; I signed the cheques for the purchase of stock and acted as Vincent's secretary. As the land rights issue developed, there was a lot of correspondence to deal with. Jenny befriended the women—the strikers had their families with them, and at times the community numbered more than 200 people—and she was given a 'skin name' and adopted by a family.

The conditions were the toughest I'd ever experienced. We lived in rough sheds made of scrap galvanised iron covered by branches—unbearably hot in the summer and awash in the Wet. Our shed was one of the best, with a floor composed of stones, but that didn't make much difference. The Wet was heavy that year, and with the rain, large centipedes came in. The kerosene fridge in the camp centre rarely

worked; we had no power and the only communication with
the outside world was by unreliable high-frequency radio.
The people wanted their land back, and they were prepared
to put up with hardship and disease to make their point.

I doubled as the station mechanic and my Toyota was
often the only workable vehicle.[1] In such a remote place,
working vehicles were more precious than gold. Another
vehicle that assumed legendary status was Brian Manning's
Bedford truck, which brought supplies down from Darwin.
Brian was a Darwin waterfront worker who was instrumental
in helping the Gurindji in the mid 1960s, some seven years
before I arrived on the scene.

The mail came in twice a week on Conair's DC3 and
we'd go to the airstrip to collect the bags, empty them out
onto the dirt floor in the central bush shelter, and I'd read the
letters out loud. Frank Hardy was still a hero to the Gurindji
and I wrote many letters urging him to visit. He never did
and rarely replied. When he did reply, I read out his letters
to a still, very respectful audience. Until you're in a situation
like that, you don't realise what power the ability to read and
write gives you. Over time I just naturally fell into the habit
of putting my construction on the letters, giving them my
own nuances and spin. The people would ask my opinion on
the matters that came up and I'd say, 'Oh, I think we should
just ignore this, and we should go ahead with that.' It gave
me a lot of influence and I liked the feeling that I was doing
something worthwhile. I don't know how long I would've
lasted as a gardener.

I realise now that I was very arrogant at times; I was sure
I could cope with whatever came up. The other side of this
was that I became intolerant of whites who came in simply to
observe or study what was happening, without (as I saw it) putting anything back in. Racists targeted me because of my iden-
tification with the Gurindji. I wrote letters that were published

in the local Katherine paper, *The Informer*, and had to watch my step when in town. White people were worried: what would happen to the cattle industry if the big operators, such as Vestey, pulled out? If the Gurindji got their land, what claims might follow? I was challenged in pubs. I tried to talk my way out of these situations, but sometimes there were fights.

Opposition to the Gurindji and their supporters took various forms. Attempts were made to sow dissent within the camp. Not long after my arrival, my father came up to Wattie Creek to visit. He'd always been interested in Aboriginal arts and crafts, and also wanted to see how his errant son was doing. One night, as dusk settled over the camp, a Toyota loaded with beer rolled in. It was driven by Van Der Build, the local Wave Hill policeman, accompanied by Len Hayes, the brother of the Wave Hill station manager, and Sabu Singh, a contract cattle musterer of Aboriginal and Indian descent.

Gurindji elder Pincher Numiari took me aside. 'Going to be trouble,' he said. 'Best you get out of the camp for the night.'

We took his advice and retreated to the edge of the camp but my father, stubborn man that he was, stayed. Before long I saw the three men who'd brought the beer shoving my father around, pushing him and shouting, 'Your son's a bloody southern shit-stirrer and you both should get out of the Territory!' There were no weapons involved and they weren't actually hitting him. My father wasn't hurt but he was very frightened, distressed and humiliated, and left the camp soon after. Those three wanted to drive a wedge between the Gurindji and whites like me. They were saying, 'We're your real mates and here's the beer to prove it.'

There were other incidents—provocations and threats— all motivated by racism and fear of change. We were branded as 'do-gooders', 'southern troublemakers' and 'nigger-lovers'. A common accusation was that we were communists. It was a long way from the quiet of the university lecture room and laboratory. I was reminded of that world, though, when my PhD certificate, neatly rolled up in its cardboard tube, arrived by post. It was an incongruous object in that desolate place.

There were problems with funding and directing the money to the right ends. Territory laws operated in favour of whites rather than blacks. For example, only pastoralists were permitted to own high-calibre rifles. To kill cattle for beef, the Aborigines had to use .22 rifles, which was a messy and cruel business. I tried to send them my cut-down .303 hunting rifle (which would have been illegal) but it mysteriously disappeared in the post somewhere between Katherine and Wave Hill.

Many years later, I was amazed to see, in Katherine, at the main southern intersection of the Stuart Highway, a larger-than-life statue of Sabu Singh that the Northern Territory Cattleman's Association had sponsored, on the basis he was a renowned stockman and pioneer. I thought him a poor choice for recognition as part of an industry built on honest Aboriginal labour. It seemed to me yet another example of the facts of Aboriginal history being overwritten by the white man.

★ ★ ★

My time among the Gurindji came to a sudden and unexpected end. Jenny had enough of roughing it after a while and began spending most of her time in Katherine. She sent down, via the twice-weekly Conair flight, food parcels to relieve the monotony of beef, beef and more beef.

I was in Katherine on station business when we both ran into James Powell, an American who was a Vietnam vet and, apparently, more charismatic than me. Powell was camping alongside us at the Katherine low-level caravan park. He'd grown up on a farm in Oklahoma, and I was impressed by his extensive knowledge of horses and station work. He, in turn, was curious about Wave Hill and wanted to know more, so came back with us for a visit. Powell was an instant hit with the community, but was an even bigger hit with Jenny, who told me the bad news with a swift, 'He's terrific, you're not much, and I'm leaving.' Before I could argue, she ended our ten years, climbed up on the back of his Honda 450 motorbike and they roared off down the Stuart Highway, headed for Mt Isa. (There is a sequel to this story, which I'll get to.)

For nearly two years, through one summer and two wet seasons, I'd given the job at Wattie Creek all I had. I didn't learn the Gurindji language, but I took a strong interest in their culture and the massive injustice they had been subjected to. It was tough physically and emotionally but also rewarding in many ways, and I thought myself something of a hero for sticking at it and earning the people's respect. But that self-image fell apart completely when Jenny left. I collapsed in a heap, and couldn't work or sleep; I was a liability and the Gurindji didn't need a passenger. Vincent Lingiari advised me to get away and sort myself out. I left for Adelaide.

Things there weren't good at all. I thought I'd be welcomed as a hero returning from the front; instead, many of my university friends had moved on. Worse, some drew attention to what they described as the arrogant and patronising letters I'd written about my important role in this land rights struggle, yet here I was back in town, and falling apart just because my relationship had broken up. My parents had separated by this time and I didn't get much sympathy there, either; my mother said she'd always thought things would fail with Jenny. I knew I had to get out of Adelaide. Then I got an invitation from Barry Frommelt, who I'd known at Flinders and who had visited me at Wave Hill. Come to Melbourne and start again, he said.

SIX

Melbourne, women and the Outback again

I write of the Northern Territory of Australia, problem child of empire, land of an over-shadowed past and an ever-shining future of eternal promise that never comes true ...

Ernestine Hill, *The Territory:
The Classic Saga of Australia's Far North*

Women have been pivotal to the directions my life has taken, and never more so than during the year and a bit I spent in Melbourne. I got a job as a tram conductor and fell in with an inner-city crowd that was interested and active in the Aboriginal rights cause. I had my Wave Hill credentials and the people in Melbourne didn't know how badly it had all ended.

I became involved with a woman named Virginia, who intrigued me because she was the total opposite of Jenny. She was a radical feminist, who wore overalls and was committed to separatist sexual politics—opposed to monogamy, and supportive of homosexuality and bisexuality. In early 1975, this intrigued me. She was a journalist, writing for radical papers like the *Nation Review* and *Digger*. Virginia was ambivalent about having a relationship with any male, let alone me, but thought we might be able to work things out if I were willing to change. So I did change—I modified my language, stopped the sexist expressions and conformed to this new style of relationship; sensitive and enlightened and well before my time. The relationship went along quite well for a few months and then I got a letter from Jenny.

She was in Mount Isa, James Powell was in gaol, and she was broke. She said it had been a mistake breaking up with me and she wanted us to get back together. It was a total shock; I thought it was over and had tried hard to forget her, but I somehow cobbled some money together for her airfare to Melbourne. I wanted her back and, since Virginia was so liberated, I thought something might be worked out. Jenny came, stayed a week, became pretty miserable and decided again that it was off, and so I paid for her to fly back to Mount Isa. She was there a fortnight, came back again to Melbourne and this time she stayed.

So I was in a two-way relationship and, strangely, the women decided they wanted to meet. I wasn't there, but apparently they got on well, and have spoken fondly of each other ever since. Then James Powell came to Melbourne, saw what was going on and erupted. He smashed up my Toyota, then threatened to kill me and I had to get the police involved. Jenny decided she had to get right away and took off to Kalgoorlie, eventually moving on to Perth.

I still had strong feelings for Jenny though, and when I got a message from Perth that she'd met someone new, I thought I'd make a last-ditch attempt to get her back. I borrowed Virginia's old AJS 350 motorbike, fixed it up and set off for Perth. It was a hell of a ride over the unsealed stretch of road across the Nullarbor; the corrugations were horrific and you couldn't avoid them. I travelled with another couple of bike riders, whose machines broke down. I made it to Perth, only to find Jenny well and truly on her feet. She'd teamed up with Jay Harman, the wealthy Perth entrepreneur and financier of the Rajneesh (Orange People) sect, and was by then installed in his Trigg penthouse. They eventually married, had a child and divorced, but that visit to the west effectively ended the Jenny chapter in my life.

On the way back to Melbourne, the bike broke down and had to be freighted back in horse transport while I hitched a ride in the truck. But on arrival, Virginia announced that she didn't want our live-in relationship to be sexual any more.

While all this was going on, I was still working on the trams, with a view to driving taxis. You were supposed to have a good geographical knowledge of Melbourne to get a cab licence and I thought tram conducting would help. However, after a year at the South Melbourne depot, I knew a lot about the Moreland to St Kilda route but little else. I did, however, meet a lot of different people in that job and mostly I enjoyed it.

In many ways, things were more free and easy then. I'd often carry a little transistor radio in my conductor's bag, as I'd always had an observer's interest in boxing and admired the courage of the fighters, and used to listen to the major fights. On the day of the 'thriller in Manila' fight between Muhammad Ali and Joe Frazier, a bunch of people travelling on the South Melbourne tram clustered around me to listen too. These days the conductors are gone, and no one entertains the passengers like that.

I eventually got my taxi driver's licence, but only worked driving yellow cabs for a few days, long enough to make me realise what a difficult job it was. I remember one night when a passenger asked to be taken to Richmond and then abused me and said he wasn't going to pay. As luck would have it, we were in Swan Street and only a few hundred metres from the police station. I accelerated suddenly so he couldn't get out, pulled up outside the station and asked again for the fare. He paid up.

Around this time, I went on a black rights march and met up again with Jean Cully, a much-loved nurse who occasionally visited Wave Hill. She'd always spoken about her daughter, Paddy, who was also on the march, and we were introduced.

Paddy had an unusual background, and was back in Australia after spending some time in Scotland. She made it clear she wanted to return there as soon as she could.

I was intrigued by Paddy's stories, and a relationship started that was to last over a decade and resulted in the birth of Philip Junior, my only child, in Alice Springs in 1977. Paddy was subject to black moods, had a strained relationship with her mother, and our temperaments meant we were never suited to each other. My involvement with other women, initially with Virginia—who Paddy hated, and it was mutual—and later with others, created emotional storms. Virginia threw me out of her flat, and tossed my stuff, including a splendid jumper Paddy had knitted from homespun yarn, out into the gutter. It was time to leave Melbourne.

Paddy and I set off north. The plan was for me to go to back to the Territory, which she would use as a jumping-off point back to Scotland. Without the problems caused by other women the relationship improved. It was a very slow trip, moving some days, other days just camping in the bush and it took us over a month to reach the Northern Territory border; Philip must have been conceived on the way. We did eventually arrive in Alice, totally broke, and I got a job unloading and unpacking freight in the railway yard of the old narrow-gauge Ghan. Then I answered an advertisement in the *Centralian Advocate*, calling for applications for the position of ranger with the Northern Territory Parks and Wildlife Service. I got the job and spent the next six years as a ranger, working first at Simpson's Gap. At the interview I realised that while my PhD wasn't highly regarded, my eighteen months on a cattle station was. I eventually got the job of southern mobile ranger, based in Alice Springs, but spent my time travelling hundreds of kilometres to the various parks up and down the centre of the Territory.

In this time my relationship with Paddy went through many phases. Philip was born in Alice Springs Hospital, and initially, as our relationship was floundering, put up for adoption, but then quickly reclaimed. It was clear to us both that it wasn't working and Paddy decided to continue with her long-planned trip to Scotland. I decided to go along for the ride, and then formally left them at Edinburgh Airport. We kept in touch though, and when I heard that she'd taken a job in China, at Kunming University, I took the opportunity to visit them both. It was a great trip—days across China by train on my own, re-meeting my four-year-old son, who was now at school, speaking Chinese, and once again enjoying the time with his mother. We began talking once again about her coming back to Australia. She did return, but it was never going to work and the Alice Springs relationship was toxic. I was repartnered with a new Jenni, and really didn't want to resume family life. There were incessant fights and misery and eventually Paddy left town and started work on Central Australian Aboriginal settlements at Papunya and Haasts Bluff. Although I would occasionally visit for weekends, her eventual permanent relocation to Scotland surprised no one and finally brought to an end a difficult relationship which—except for Philip—I regret to this day.

Philip was to return to Australia for his high school years. Paddy had established an Australian base in Hobart, the city she seemed fondest of, and although she was in and out of the country, Philip was able to finish high school and went on to the University of Tasmania, eventually earning a PhD in chemistry. Armed with his chemistry expertise, he initially worked at a winery but is now back in academe, at his alma mater. He lives in Hobart with his wife and three young boys. We're on good terms and see each other when I'm down there. Like me, he enjoys his craft beer—I'm a bit of a beer snob and will go out of my way to get the right India Pale Ale. He, on the other hand, knows the chemistry of brewing, which is knowledge that I envy. We have that, and scientific language in common; as to his politics, I just don't know.

To this day, I'm not entirely sure what Philip thinks of my work. It's not an issue we've discussed in detail. When I'm in Hobart campaigning or running euthanasia workshops he occasionally comes along to my public meetings. I'm sure he doesn't disagree, but like many, probably wonders why anyone would keep on with an issue like this for so long and with so little obvious gain. He uses his mother's last name, which has provided him with a degree of anonymity, although staff at the university know he's my son and on some occasions, such as the conferring of his PhD, the media have also made reference to it. While my relationship with Philip is more that of friends than of father and son, he is a wonderful grandson to my mother, Gwen. He calls her regularly and visits her in Adelaide. One thing Paddy did do was instil in him a strong sense of family, maybe because her family was so fractured. On his twenty-fifth birthday, Philip inherited part of the substantial estate of his maternal great-aunt. That financial freedom has produced a young man who doesn't have much to be angry about and I see him today as a contented father and husband who dotes on his family.

★ ★ ★

I came to love the life and the bush in central Australia when I worked as a ranger. The MacDonnell Ranges are stunning and I felt lucky to be there. Tourists I came into contact with would see me going about my work in a leisurely fashion and comment that I had the best job in the world. It didn't always feel like it, when I was cleaning out pit toilets, or being bitten by centipedes when camping out, or scraping down barbecue plates, but mostly I agreed with them. I visited the small parks scattered over the vast area that didn't have resident staff. That meant cleaning up, mending fences and controlling feral animals; I had the skills for that.

I'd always enjoyed camping and it was a life that suited me—I'd roll out of my swag in the morning, put in a radio report about where I was and what I was doing, and then set about doing things at my own pace. I loved the freedom. I also got on well with most of the people I worked with, particularly Bob Darken, the senior ranger at Simpson's Gap. He was an ex-wool classer, ex-policeman, ex-pastoralist, at one time a mate of iconic Australian actor Chips Rafferty, and a rough, idiosyncratic Territorian.

But I got off to a rocky start. In my first week on the job, when I was still on probation, I ran up against one of the things that incense civil libertarians—an accusation is made that damages you and that your employers act upon, but one that you are not permitted to see. A letter critical of me came from Mike Reed, another ranger, and, once in the system, this letter immediately became 'privileged information'. It wasn't until twenty years later (when it was anonymously faxed to me in Darwin) that I learned what Reed's specific allegations were. Some were minor, like that my vehicle had dripped oil in the Katherine Low Level Reserve camping ground where he was head ranger when I came into town from Wave Hill. However, he also denounced me to the Parks and Wildlife Service as a 'political troublemaker', who wanted to join the service to further the interests of the blacks in their efforts to take over control of Territory national parks. He accused me of being a communist, of having been funded at Wave Hill by unions that were themselves financed from Russia. (Interestingly, I recently met a researcher in Tasmania, who was a PhD student with the historian Henry Reynolds, doing work on the Wave Hill strike. She told me of an ASIO file on me, alleging that I was a member of the Australian Communist Party. Although I have often been in sympathy with their aims, I have never been a member of the CPA.) Finally, Reed claimed that I had lied about my tertiary qualifications, just to get the job. There was nothing in the letter about the quality of the work I'd been doing.

On hearing of this letter, Bob told me to cease working. 'If any of that is true,' he said, 'I want you off my park.' When he found that I wasn't allowed even to see the letter, or to be given any real chance to counter it, his sense of fair play was offended and he swung back to my side and stayed there.

It wasn't always overt, but it was always there—that underlying fear that the advancement of Aboriginal rights would ultimately override white control of life in the Territory. Judging by Reed, this view could fester for years.

And the mud stuck. Over the next few years, I wasn't given promotions I was in line for and my Parks and Wildlife career was stymied. Meanwhile, Mike Reed moved steadily up through the ranks and became the director of the service. He was being groomed for a political career and eventually became Deputy Chief Minister under Marshall Perron. I would encounter Reed again ten years later, when I returned to the Territory as a junior doctor. I would see him in a very different context but, in a way, nothing had changed: he still represented the most reactionary elements of Northern Territory politics and society.

During these rangering years, I joined in the protest activities against the Pine Gap base, 18 kilometres from Alice Springs. With lawyer John Reeves (now a judge of the Federal Court), I founded the group Concerned Citizens of Alice Springs and began publishing a regular newsletter critical of the American presence there. With others, I occasionally camped outside Pine Gap and probed the perimeter, and we constantly voiced our concern about the secrecy of the installation. It was different sides of the same triangle, as far as I was concerned—weapons development, uranium mining, foreign military bases and, later, nuclear submarines were all symbols of American imperialism, all obstacles to a peaceful and just world.

* * *

Looking for other satisfactions while my rangering career was in the doldrums, I joined the army reserve. This involved two three-week semi-military assignments a year, mostly out in the bush, learning new skills. You got double pay if you were working for the government, which I welcomed because the Parks and Wildlife pay was low. After one of these operations—an advanced four-wheel-drive training course in Arnhem Land—I arrived back at the Larrakeyah barracks in Darwin. We were preparing to celebrate what had been an interesting ten days, and I was sitting on a large Esky on the back of a stationary army International 4WD truck, looking forward to a few beers. Suddenly, the truck started up, turned abruptly and I was thrown off. I got hit over the head by the aforementioned full Esky of beer and landed badly on the kerb; my right heel broke away from my foot and my lower leg was a bloody mess.

I was taken to what was then Darwin Hospital at Myilly Point, only a few hundred metres from the barracks. I remember asking the admitting doctor whether I'd broken my leg.

'You'll wish you had,' he said.

He was right. It took three operations to repair the injury, which was to the joint that controls the lateral movement of the foot. Normally, your ankle bends when you walk but you need lateral movement for stability when your foot strikes uneven ground. Many people who have suffered the same injury experience constant pain when walking on rough ground. My pain comes and goes, but of course the injury put an immediate end to rangering, as walking in rough country is a big part of the job.

I was in Darwin Hospital for some time, and then in a little RAAF hospital in Darwin before I was flown down to Alice Springs Hospital. I was finally released on crutches and spent weeks slowly doing weight-bearing exercises. After each operation, I would be back on crutches, wearing special boots to shift the weight up my foot. I was surprised at how slow the recovery was. I went to the Alice Springs swimming pool twice a day; I would hobble across it, taking advantage of the buoyancy, trying to avoid the lap swimmers. Then I'd be off to physio at the hospital. It was months before I could put my whole weight on my right foot. More than thirty years later, I still walk with a limp and my foot always gives me trouble if I walk too much.

It wasn't exactly a mid-life crisis—or certainly not a psychological one—but it was clear I would need a new and less physical occupation.

SEVEN

Medicine in the Big City

*The 'e' word had never been mentioned at Sydney
Medical School ...*

Philip Nitschke, 2011

I'd never lost interest in the idea of a career in medicine. Now,
laid up, recovering from my accident, I thought I should
finally apply. I sent off applications to every medical school in
the country. I believed my best chance would be at Newcastle,
where they had a new and innovative admission policy, based
more on a person's character and experience, and so more suitable for a 'mature age' applicant such as myself. I was surprised
to be offered places, for the academic year starting 1982, at
Sydney, Monash and Adelaide; Newcastle ignored me.

A few months before, I'd met Marlies as I was limping
about Alice Springs after one of my foot operations. German-
born Marlies had come to Australia, some years earlier, to
work as a nurse. She was in Alice Springs on a working
holiday for several months, doing shifts at the hospital, and
we met at an anti-Pine Gap rally. She was very much the new
girl in town. At the time we met, she had a partner, Henry,
in Melbourne and I was just about to leave Alice and go to
medical school. We went out camping, which she loved, and
a relationship started that was to last another ten years. When
we left Alice, we planned to take the very long route across the

Tanami, through Gurindji country to Katherine and down to Sydney. It was to be a great trip but, after a week of being flood-bound on the Tanami Track, we were forced back to the Stuart Highway. After a tearful farewell in Sydney, Marlies continued on to Melbourne and, soon after that, left for a long-planned year overseas with Henry. We stayed in contact for the whole twelve months she was away, with letters and phone calls to and from Sydney and Germany. Her absence would make first-year medicine particularly difficult for me, but with her return to Sydney in early 1983, as I started my second year, our relationship became firmly established.

I'd never lived in Sydney before, and the idea of starting something completely new in a new city quite appealed to me. Also, the Sydney Medical School course took five years, while all the others were six, and at my age— thirty-five—six years would have felt like a big piece out of my life. I was lucky with timing, in that I undertook medicine when university courses were still free, but I knew I'd have to work, as my PhD made me ineligible for any government living allowance. By this time, I'd begun a compensation case against the army, and had hopes of a settlement that would help get me through medical school and into this new career.

It was standard practice then for medical courses to have basic physics and chemistry units in their first year. I applied for exemption from physics and was refused. This was the first time I struck against an attitude at Sydney that would increasingly irritate me: that their medical degree was so prestigious that no outside qualifications could be of any consequence. I applied for a part-time tutorship in the School of Physics and, with my PhD in hand, was duly appointed. When the student tutorial lists went up, however, I found I was rostered as a student in my own tutorial. I took this information to the Dean of the Medical Faculty and finally they deigned to grant me an exemption from first-year physics.

My biggest stroke of luck during medical school was getting virtually free accommodation. Sydney is, and was, an expensive place to live and I was going to be on a very tight budget. Before I left the Territory, I met Gil Scrine, who was making his award-winning film *Home on the Range*, about the Pine Gap base. I got to know him quite well and he told me that if I were ever in Sydney, I could use the houseboat he had moored at Balmain, as he was going to be off filming somewhere. I took him up on this and stayed in that rather nice setting for a while. Rowing out at night, studying by kerosene light, living illegally on Sydney Harbour. He also gave me the use of his VW Beetle so I could commute to the university. It was a pleasant, but impractical way to live, and when in the middle of my first year the offer of a place in a Camperdown squat came up, I jumped at the chance.

I had met up with another Alice Springs connection, Des Carne, who was squatting in the unoccupied South Sydney Women's Hospital. It was perfect: in Camperdown, walking distance to the university, and free. I stayed there for a year, and had a huge space, one of the old operating theatres, all to myself. When it was finally sold at the end of my first year, the new owners decided to demolish it, and a number of us simply moved across the street, to what had been the nurses' quarters. With the power and water connected, and with the cooperation of the owner, a church affiliate of some kind, we were well set up. Vandals had caused damage, and had stripped some of the lead and other things of value, so we were welcomed as rent-free caretakers. I stayed there for the next three years and Marlies moved in.

Still, I can't say I was altogether happy doing medicine at Sydney. My friendships with my fellow students weren't close ones. At thirty-five years of age I didn't have much in common with them, most of whom, I thought, had had pretty sheltered lives. I also found the rote learning of medical facts boring, but I still sweated over the exams, even though they were mostly multiple-choice, tick-the-boxes style.

That said, the actual content of the course was everything I'd hoped for, especially in the first few years. Like many doctors, I'm fascinated by the complexities of the human body and especially its interaction with the environment. I was, and am, particularly interested in the history and philosophy of medicine, topics that continue to be highly relevant to my work today.

Living in Sydney I missed the Territory, though. At one point, the city overwhelmed me and I took off to go bush, about as far as you can go. The Gibson Desert is a remote area of about 15 million hectares on the Western Australia–Northern Territory border. I'd always wanted to go there and it provided the perfect antidote to Sydney. I went out to Jupiter Well, a dot on the map of the Gibson, and didn't see anyone or talk to anyone for over a month. I didn't go out of my way to avoid people; it was just that no one came along. I'd get up every day at sunrise and clamber up the sand dune nearest the camp, and could see the whole 360 degrees of the horizon. It was an amazing and humbling experience.

For a period of about four days, I could see smoke on the horizon and it moved a little to the east each day. That meant there were people still out there, although the last of the traditional Pintupi people had supposedly walked out of the desert into Aboriginal communities in the mid 1960s. It pleased me to think that there were still some people out there, out of contact and unaffected by Western civilisation.

Jupiter Well was really a soak, and I dug it out so that I could get water. I also thought I should do something to mark my stay. I stamped my name and the date, and something about digging out the well, on an aluminium plate, drove a star picket into the ground and wired the plate to it. I was imitating Len Beadell, a surveyor, bushman and road builder in the years after World War II. He started out making access roads to the infamous Maralinga atomic test site, but continued to build a network of roads in central Australia. His most notable road is the Gunbarrel Highway, which runs right through the Gibson. He wrote a number of books about his experiences, telling how he'd hammered his name and other information onto metal plates, shot holes in them with his revolver, and bolted them to 44-gallon drums filled with cement.

About twenty years after my visit, I got an email from a bloke who'd recently been at Jupiter Well and had dug the well out, just as I had. He'd found the plaque I'd left, recognised the name Nitschke as associated with euthanasia and wondered if I'd had anything to do with it. He sent a photograph, and there it was—the marker I'd made, still intact. Many of Beadell's markers have been souvenired, or acquired by museums, and there's a plan to replace them. I wonder whether my plaque has been souvenired by now; I'd like to go back and see.

Looking back on that experience in the desert, I realise that I was looking for more than just a break from Sydney. Ever since the episodes with headaches and chest pains, and my brush with psychiatry, I'd been subject to the utter terror that goes with thinking you are dying from some terrible disease. This form of hypochondria allows you to slide down into a cycle of worry about symptoms, which allows more symptoms to develop. For me, sometimes there have been real triggers and real fears. For example, there were many lepers at Wave Hill. I'd noticed that quite a number of the people were wearing shoes, which was unusual for the Gurindji, and I wondered why. I found out that they were being treated at the East Arm Leprosarium in Darwin. With leprosy, you lose sensation in your feet and hands and so become subject to injuries like camp fire burns—you simply don't notice them. This leaves you vulnerable to infections, and that's when gangrene can set in.

In Alice, when I was rangering, I began noticing changes to sensation in my feet—peripheral neuropathy, which is a disturbance of the nerves and interference with normal sensation. My first thought was leprosy; the incubation period for its development seemed about right and I immediately began to panic. I then spent weeks seeing doctors with little satisfaction, until I finally found Trevor Cutler at the Aboriginal health centre, who had some experience of the condition. He examined my feet and quickly dismissed my feared diagnosis. I forget what he attributed the neuropathy to, but he told me to forget it and almost immediately the trouble went away.

Over the years, I've struggled with these demons and wonder occasionally, why me? What was it about my parents or upbringing that made me vulnerable? No one else I knew had this problem, and rarely was there any sympathy. In fact, when I elected to do medicine, it was at the back of my mind that I could educate myself out of my fears and phobias. Unfortunately, the plan failed spectacularly. At medical school, you learn about a whole lot of new diseases worse than any you've ever heard of, and what you think might be wrong with you expands exponentially. I think that by going alone out into the desert I was looking for some kind of quasi-spiritual experience to help me straighten out my thinking. It may have worked for a time but the hypochondria persists and it's been one of the main causes of conflict in many of my relationships with women; living with someone who regularly thinks they're dying can be intolerable.

★ ★ ★

I had to spend time in Alice Springs when the case involving my broken foot finally came to court. The process had started years earlier, when I was limping down Todd Street and ran into lawyer Peter McQueen. There'd been a small piece in the paper about my army accident, which was how he knew about it.

'How's it going?' he asked.

I answered, 'Not too damn well.'

'What're they doing for you?'

'Oh, that's all good. I'm getting all this medical help for free. Everything's covered.'

'What else are they doing?'

'What else should they be doing?'

'I think they'd better do more than that.'

He invited me to his office and told me I had a good torts action for negligence against the federal government. I was a bit taken aback because I thought, and still think, that people should be responsible for their own behaviours. He pointed out that my career as a ranger was finished and that I'd have ongoing medical problems. I wasn't too worried about the future, as I believed I could find something else to do, but he persuaded me that I'd be foolish not to provide for myself. I agreed to start legal action against the army.

My lawyer friend John Reeves advised me to get a good barrister. Lew Wyvill from Brisbane, who'd just become a QC, was suggested. It was a risky business because if I lost the case, I'd have to pay his fees and the court costs. I put up my house—a very modest one I'd bought for $29 000 in The Gap, a suburb of Alice Springs—as a surety and Lew joined the team.

I was alarmed when I met him. I had expected to talk things over with him but he just gave me just a cursory hand-shake before proceeding to rip into me. He tore my account of what had happened to shreds, which left me confused, angry and upset. I remember thinking, *This lawyer should have been brought into Alice in a cage.*

Then his manner changed. He said, 'This isn't a game. It could get hard in there tomorrow and I wanted you to get the feel of just what can happen if lawyers start in on you.'

It was a good tactic and it did prepare me. Lew was friendly to me out of the court room, but ruthless in it. He hammered the army's lawyer, who didn't seem to have researched the matter very well, stressing the duty of care and negligence and picking holes in their defence. When the afternoon session was over, Lew came to me and told me the army was making an offer.

I said, 'What do I do?'

He said, 'In cases like this, I usually say if the offer is less than you expected, go on with the case; if it's more, grab it. I have to tell you, though, that if this goes on, you'll have to charter a plane to get me back to Brisbane, where I've got another trial running. I don't know what your expectation was.'

'I was hoping for something like ten thousand dollars,' I said.

'The offer's a hundred thousand and they'll meet the costs.'

That made for an easy decision.

I'd accumulated debts over my three years of medicine, and was able to clear them and have a good sum of money left over to get me through my degree. However, on getting my payout, I found I couldn't resist the appeal of having a long break from medicine. I decided to defer, which surprised a lot of people and, even more surprisingly, I then spent most of the remaining money buying a sailing boat named *Squizz*, a cutter-rigged steel sloop. Marlies was keen. Having come with me on trips back to the Territory, she had also accompanied me on one where we drove my old army 4WD truck from Alice, across the Gibson and down the Canning Stock Route, to Perth. We did a sailing course in Fremantle but couldn't find the right yacht there or in Adelaide. Eventually, we bought *Squizz* in Melbourne.

With medicine temporarily deferred, I threw myself into learning how to sail on Port Phillip Bay. I started slowly, with a series of small trips, and then around the Bass Strait islands and on to Tasmania. Marlies came along some of the time. What I hadn't known when I bought the boat, however, was just how seasick I'd get in rough weather. Once, I became trapped at Lady Barron on Flinders Island. The

Squizz couldn't perform upwind, and I made three attempts to sail west out of Franklin Sound but made almost no headway. I talked to some of the local sailors and they thought the *Squizz* could make it through the notorious Pot Boil to the east, but only if I picked the right time and right conditions, and that's what I did.

I had some magical moments sailing, such as finding a safe anchorage at an island, rowing ashore and taking in the unspoiled beauty around me. It was something like being in the desert, although if I had to choose, the desert would win.

Before the year was out, I was taking a break in Hobart, moored at Constitution Dock, when I got a radiophone call. Sydney University was threatening to cancel my course unless I immediately returned to complete the degree. I'd deferred and deferred, and now they'd run out of patience. Having little choice, I sailed back up Australia's east coast and found an anchorage in Botany Bay.

The final year of a medical course is mostly spent in hospitals and there was intense competition to get allocated an inner-city hospital, so as not to have to spend hours commuting to and from places like Westmead and Concord in Sydney's west. I was lucky and assigned to Royal Prince Alfred Hospital in Camperdown. That final year I remember having lectures on ophthalmology from Fred Hollows, who was well on his way to becoming the legend he is now.

The squat had gone by that stage, but I had another stroke of luck when I met up with yet another Territory contact. He was something of an intellectual but with a dubious past and about to serve a period in prison for his white-collar crime. He was the only person I've ever met who has written a regular newspaper column about the game of chess. Anyway, he was off to prison, but had a place in Bellevue Hill that needed house-sitting, and was I interested? I was and moved in.

I went back to Alice as often as I could. Whenever there was a break, I'd be down at Central Station, waving my half-price student ticket and going Sydney–Melbourne, Melbourne–Adelaide, Adelaide–Alice. I even made one memorable trip hidden in the back of a friend's car. It was summer and I was particularly broke and needed to get back to Sydney. So I convinced a mate who was taking his car on the Ghan from Alice to Adelaide to let me stow away. I climbed into the car in mid afternoon, just before it was to be loaded, and lay concealed under a blanket in the back seat. As sweat dripped from every pore, I seriously thought I'd have to give in, reveal myself and confess. Finally, at dusk, I felt movement and within minutes the train pulled out of Alice Springs and we were away. Thank Christ. I'd had the wherewithal to bring a six-pack and a cooked chicken with me, not to mention a few litres of water, most of which I'd drunk while under the blanket. The sunset that night was breathtaking, as was the following morning's sunrise. A 360-degree view of the Outback, the ranges, the immense vastness. One of life's unforgettable moments.

With medicine now almost finished, the issue of organising an internship came up. I wanted to get out of New South Wales and back to the Territory, so applied for the Alice Springs Hospital, but was knocked back; this wasn't because of any earlier troubles but because this hospital was too small to take any interns. Instead, I got a placement at Royal Darwin.

EIGHT

The Top End

I head a little further north each year
Leave the cities behind, out of sight, out of mind

Graeme Connors, 'A Little Further North'

I'm keen on country music, so, at the beginning of 1989 as I drove north to start my new life at Royal Darwin Hospital, I had the gentle lilt of Graeme Connors' 'A Little Further North' echoing through my old Toyota Landcruiser. I was simply so pleased to be going back to where I felt I belonged—albeit 1500 kilometres further north, up the track.

When I started work in the hospital, I was one of fourteen interns from different medical schools all over Australia. Sydney University's claim to be 'the best' was quickly shown to be rubbish—some of the new doctors seemed as well trained as Sydney graduates, and quite a few were better.

As an intern, you're very low in any hospital's pecking order, and some of the medical and nursing staff will take any opportunity to show you up for all you don't know. You usually start off in the general fields of surgery or medicine and then move into more specialised areas. For some reason, in Darwin I was thrown straight into orthopaedics, about which I knew bugger all. Steve Baddeley (the surgeon who had operated on my heel many years earlier) was the head of the section, and as intern, I had to trail around after him and the other orthopaedic registrars and resident medical officers (RMOs), picking up what I could. On day three, the section's senior registrar, Robin Cripps, told me to see a certain patient, and take blood so his electrolytes could be determined. I could see that the patient had little time left; I tried to talk to him but he was almost comatose.

I would have had to use a needle to get blood from his veins and I asked the sister what the point of this was.

'Because Robin wants it,' was the answer.

I thought, *I'm not going to do this*, and I went back to Cripps and said it was a waste of time.

He said, 'You're a fucking intern and you'll do what you're fucking told.'

Baddeley was present and he just nodded; I was being shown how the system works and where the power lies. So I had to rush off and stick a needle into this dying patient.

In that orthopaedic world, Steve Baddeley was god. He drove around in a sports car, and ruled. He set the agenda, and had us all working at weekends, doing ward rounds. He'd put us under the microscope: 'What's your view of so and so? Have you done this, have you done that?' I found him hard going at times but gradually our relationship improved, and he was to be very important years later, when the euthanasia issue broke.

Boxing—amateur and some professional—was important in Darwin and I got involved in a roundabout way. I took a phone call one day when working in the accident and emergency section, from Boyd Scully at the Territory Boxing Association. He asked if there was a doctor willing to be present at a few forthcoming fights, as the law required. Apparently, the doctor who usually officiated wasn't available. I asked the medicos if anyone was interested, but got a storm of censure back, with the registrar saying, 'Boxing's not a sport; you set out to do injury. It's against AMA policy, you know.' This annoyed me. These people (mostly Aboriginal) were trying to stage a popular event and they'd have to call it off if a doctor wouldn't stand in. So I agreed to do it.

I found it fascinating as I learnt the rules and regulations about how the fights were to be conducted. I had to examine the boxers before the bouts, to ensure they were fit to fight and, during the bouts, check on any developing medical problems—cuts, blood in the eyes, severe bruising. The amateurs fought three three-minute rounds and wore headgear, and the trainers and referees kept a close eye on them. The fights were stopped if a boxer got into trouble and I thought it generally ran well. One of my jobs was to help rule exactly when a fight should be stopped.

Things were rougher in the professional fights, which went on for much longer: up to twelve rounds; as well, there was no headgear and there was always money involved. I remember one fight, at the Nightcliff pub, where things got ugly. One of the boxers was clearly outclassed and the referee stopped the fight. I agreed with him, but the crowd had other ideas and erupted, throwing chairs and whatever else they could lay their hands on. I was glad I wasn't the one who'd had to announce the decision.

Most of the fighters were black and the people associated with boxing weren't from the middle-class, so I was brought into contact with a different segment of society. On occasion, when I was out of my depth with some problems concerning the fighters, I would ring doctors down south who'd had years of experience in the field, and was never let down. My involvement with Northern Territory boxing is one of my happier Darwin memories.

A spin-off from my involvement in boxing was winning, in 1990, a thousand-dollar prize in a competition the hospital ran, in which interns and junior doctors were invited to put up research proposals. The results were presented at a dinner, to which everyone was invited. After doing a lot of reading on the subject—and this was typical of me;

I'll read a lot about things I'm interested in, but not much for recreation—I built a small accelerometer (a device that can measure force) to be positioned inside a boxer's headgear to measure the speed and intensity of blows to the head. The real-time results were radio-linked to a ringside computer, which would record each punch, its time and force, as a blip on the screen. The device was designed to help with the scoring system used in boxing, as it's often hard for the naked eye to accurately judge scoring punches. It worked pretty well. I tried to interest Arthur Tunstall, the head of the Australian Amateur Boxing Association, in it, but he showed little interest in this new technology

Anyway, I won the prize, but in medical circles some people did not view the project favourably. There is a lot of hypocrisy in medicine. If you're opposed to the idea of people punching each other as sport, say so, but don't dress up your objections as being a medical matter, which many doctors did. The evidence regarding physical damage from amateur boxing is far from clear, and it needs to be compared with injury from other contact sports such as rugby, for a specific case to be made against it.

That year, I also officiated as boxing doctor at the first Arafura Games, a week-long sporting event held in Darwin every second year, and did so until recently. The games began in 1991, and, apart from their cancellation in 2003 because of the Asian bird flu, had run regularly, attracting competitors from more than thirty countries, playing a range of sports. In 2012 the CLP Territory government announced that the games would be cancelled because of the cost. Their future is now uncertain.

At the end of that second year at Royal Darwin, I decided to bring the *Squizz* to Darwin. She'd been slopping around in Botany Bay and Marlies, who was completing her naturopathy course in Sydney, would row out from time to time to do some maintenance. It's hard enough looking after

a boat when you're nearby, but a real pain when you're not.
The plan was for Marlies and me to sail her up the coast,
through the Torres Strait, to Darwin. We got to Byron Bay
and anchored. Reports of bad weather ahead started to come
in, but I'd been through rough weather in Bass Strait and
didn't take it seriously enough. We went ashore and climbed
up to the lighthouse to see the view. When we got back to
the boat, the radio weather reports were even worse and,
later that night, we started to drag the anchor.

I thought, *Bloody hell, we'd better get out of here.* With
onshore winds, we were likely to be driven ashore. It was
about 2 a.m., conditions were dreadful, and after an immense
struggle we finally managed to get the anchor up. I thought
it would be impossible to tack upwind to get out of the bay;
I'd have to motor out. And then I made one of my worst mistakes, one you read about in all the books: I managed to get
the anchor trip line caught in the propeller. That finished the
motor as soon as it started up. The only thing left was to tack,
tack, tack, slowed down by the trapped anchor held under the
hull, to fight our way out of the bay. We spent the whole night,
in drenching rain, slowly making headway till finally Byron
Bay was cleared and we could move north up the coast.

Battling along through the next day, I thought, *We'll stop
as soon as we can to sort things out*, but all the ports were closed
due to the weather. I radioed that we were in trouble, that we
couldn't anchor effectively because my large anchor was out
of action and the emergency one wouldn't do. As we crossed
the Queensland border, the coastguard at Point Danger suggested we come in to the lee of the point, that there was a
bit of protection there and they could take us off the boat.
They reckoned they could also help us by bringing out a
75-kg anchor on a jet ski. It was getting dark and we were
both exhausted. I put my goggles on one last time, and went
down, cut the trip-line free and released our trapped anchor.
We were taken to the Rainbow Bay Lifesaving Club, and I

thought that finally things were improving and the boat was safe. We were now in Queensland and a photographer from the *Gold Coast Bulletin* took a picture to illustrate the drama that was going on. Two boats were lost at sea that day: the *Rockin' Robin*, whose four crew had been seen getting into a life raft that had been dropped from a rescue aircraft, but then never seen again; and the *Banshee*, carrying two women who were sailing to New Zealand—they lost their boat, but were rescued by a Taiwanese freighter.

Marlies and I were put up in the lifesaving club and given bunks to sleep in. It was a great relief after twenty-four sleepless hours, with me being seasick the whole time. I got up in the morning and thought I'd have a look at how the boat was doing. It was gone. I couldn't believe it. Marlies came out to find me staring out to sea. We ran to the coast-guard office and broke the news, then sat around for about five hours, waiting. I was convinced the boat had gone to the bottom. Finally, search and rescue found it, way out to sea, still floating but dismasted. It must have rolled over, torn free of the big anchor, and lost its mast and all the rigging. A tremendous amount of damage. I was amazed that the *Squizz* hadn't been washed ashore but strange things happen at sea. The coastguard went out, hooked it up, and towed it in to the Southport Yacht Club.

It stayed there, a bedraggled-looking wreck and source of great interest, amongst the millionaires' yachts. For some weeks we lived in a Gold Coast motel and tried to get some basic repairs done; eventually some insurance money came in and *Squizz* was moved to where proper repairs could be carried out. The upshot was that, instead of the romantic adventure of sailing through Torres Strait to Darwin, I sold the boat and flew on to Darwin while Marlies returned to Sydney. Eventually I used what was left of the insurance money to buy another yacht, a 10-metre steel sloop *Nullagai*—a much better one, which had already been around the world.

Later, I saw a photograph of *Squizz* in a magazine that advertises boats for sale, and I once even saw her afloat in a Queensland marina. Now, though, I had dreams of sailing my new yacht, *Nullagai*, to foreign ports. I lived on the boat for a time in Darwin and sailed it occasionally on the harbour, but as my interests changed and the euthanasia issue descended upon me, I couldn't devote the time needed to maintain it properly. Eventually, it became derelict and it now sits, rusting and decaying in the jungle on my rural property at Darwin. I call it a 'monument to my failed dreams' and feel guilty about it because the previous owner and builder of this yacht took great pride in the boat. It deserved a better fate.

★ ★ ★

At the end of my intern year at Darwin hospital, Marlies and I went to Germany to spend Christmas with her family. Marlies had continued to live in Sydney, finishing a naturopathy course. During that time while I was alone in Darwin, I became involved with the visiting ophthalmology registrar, Kate. As a result, the trip to Germany did not go well. When Marlies and I returned to Australia after the holiday, the loose plan was that I would go straight back to Darwin and she would join me a few months later. However, torn as I was at having to make a choice, Kate won out. On Marlies' arrival north, I had to tell her of the dilemma. To her credit, she was having none of it and left on the next bus back to Sydney. Despite the rather shameful way I treated her in the final stages of our relationship we remain friends. She is a woman of incredible inner strength and integrity, one of the few people I've met that I would trust with my life.

The relationship with Kate was never going to work. It was another Darwin romance, an infatuation, something the hospital was renowned for. Seconded staff were often miles away from their southern homes, trapped in the staff village and surrounded by the sensory beauty of the tropics. Intense, but transitory, the relationship finally floundered after a few months as the pre-Wet build-up put everyone on edge. Kate moved back to Sydney.

Not long after this, a young paediatric registrar would appear on the scene. Like Jenny, Paddy and Marlies, Tristan would remain an integral part of my life for the next decade. As a junior hospital doctor, you don't forget some of the nicer, more experienced doctors who help you along the way— Tristan was one. We met while I was working in casualty. When seriously ill children were brought in, as a senior pae-diatric registrar Tristan was often called in for emergencies: a young child may have nearly drowned in a pool or be near to death from severe dehydration. What impressed me about Tristan was the utter calm with which she approached these chaotic medical situations where life and death were in the balance. Her ability to instil order and exude authority and assurance as the rest of us ran around in a panic was greatly admired by the casualty staff. Our professional relationship quickly became a personal one, as is so common in Darwin. Although from very different backgrounds, and of almost opposite temperaments, our relationship worked very well for a number of years.

Meanwhile, I was increasingly finding my feet at Royal Darwin Hospital. An incident that sticks in my mind is meet-ing the notorious murderer Daniel Heiss. In 1991 Daniel, and another man, Peter Kamm, were sentenced to life in prison for the 1989 murder of Dean Robinson, which took place south of Darwin when Daniel was only twenty-three. The murder was considered particularly gruesome because the shallow grave the men dug was not deep enough for Robinson's head, which was left exposed, only to be set alight and then covered with an anthill.[1]

I first became aware of Daniel Heiss when I arrived one day to commence a 6 a.m. shift in casualty and saw a rope made of knotted sheets hanging from a smashed tenth-floor window. Curiously, the rope ended at around the first floor, and I wondered what was going on. I would later learn that Daniel had used the sheets to make what would be the first of two escapes during his twenty-three-year incarceration. The audacity of the hospital escape effort caught my attention and I was very interested when I finally met Daniel, some two years later.

Daniel had come into hospital for investigation following a stomach complaint, and was handcuffed to a trolley in the examination room. I was undertaking my anaesthetic term and was sent to review him for surgery. We had a chat as I tried to take blood, which was next to impossible, since he was handcuffed to the trolley by both ankles and wrists, something I'd never seen before: total overkill. After what amounted to a stand-off, I finally convinced the prison guards to grudgingly release one of his arms. I liked Daniel—who was polite and had a good sense of humour, but sadly resigned to his plight—and I felt for him in his humiliation.

Daniel would make a second escape in 1995, and evaded police capture for twelve days, by living rough in Darwin's rural area. In typical Territory style, he came to be seen as having something of a Ned Kelly persona, with people even leaving food out for him. Given that more than two hundred police were involved in the search, this public support for Daniel says something about the resentment Territorians commonly show towards authority. I would later join the community support committee that was lobbying for Daniel's release on parole after seven failed applications and I often visited him in jail. Daniel's co-accused, Peter Kamm, was granted parole in April 2010. In my mind, locking a person up for life is a form of torture and serves no purpose. I was disgusted when the Country Liberal Party used Daniel's image for a law-and-order election campaign titled 'Life Means Life', as Daniel had done his time. He finally got parole in June

2011 and I was very pleased to have been involved in a small way. One of Daniel's paintings now hangs in my office and I see him when I'm in Darwin.

In the year I met Daniel, I was also appointed as the hospital's medical photographer, with the job of making a photographic record of wounds and injuries and documenting many of the medical cases that came through the hospital. Photographing the rare croc attacks, box-jellyfish stings and other medical phenomena, much of it in the mortuary, took up half my time; the rest was spent as a doctor in accident and emergency. Then things came unstuck. Because of my background in physics, I was also the hospital's radiation protection officer. When I arrived at work one day, I was stunned to see a notice instructing all medical staff to report for training sessions on what to do in the event of a nuclear accident and emergency. The notice went on to explain that this was necessary because the US nuclear submarine *USS Houston* was arriving in Darwin Harbour the following week. Despite being radiation protection officer, I'd heard nothing of any radiation-exposure training session, and the idea that staff could be brought up to speed on this crucial matter within twenty-four hours was ludicrous. I was critical of the nuclear industry, and a Darwin visit by an American nuclear warship looked like just another item on that country's long litany of sins.

I made a public statement as a spokesman for the newly formed Darwin branch of the 'Medical Association for the Prevention of War' and my complaints went out the same evening on ABC radio's *PM* program. Then hell broke loose. I was accused of breaching the *Public Service Act*, and the Department of Health issued a statement contradicting what I'd said about the hospital's preparedness for nuclear emergencies. Although the *USS Houston* came and went, it was to be three weeks of bitter dispute before the Northern Territory Department of Health finally apologised to me.

It was seen as a great victory, and we all thought that would be the end of it.

A few weeks later, I took the opportunity to give evidence to a Senate committee that was looking at Territorian views on disaster planning and I spoke about the hospital's unsatisfactory arrangements. The next day, my old adversary from rangering days, Mike Reed, now the Territory Health Minister, issued an ominous press release finishing with the line: 'If Dr Nitschke doesn't like the situation, I have no doubt the Royal Darwin Hospital will be able to scrape by without him.' A few days later, I got a letter from the hospital, telling me that my services as a doctor would not be required when my contract finished in two months.

This was unprecedented. Royal Darwin's doctors' contracts were always renewed, and doctors were always in short supply. There followed months of wrangling, with a threatened strike by junior doctors, inquiries into the incident from the Department of Health and the AMA, with findings suppressed for fear of libel, and finally an investigation by the Senate Privileges Committee into whether I had been discriminated against in my employment on the basis of evidence I had given under privilege. In its final report, the Senate Committee stopped short of finding this, but asserted that a remedy should follow due to 'those who have punished Dr Nitschke for what should have been his right as a citizen'.

An AMA report on the difficulties at Royal Darwin was carried out by Dr Peter Arnold of the New South Wales branch of the AMA and produced a mixed set of conclusions. There were apparently things in his report that were favourable, but also some criticism. The phrase 'enemy of the people'—the title of an Ibsen play— was used, with the implication that I fell into that category. I say 'apparently', because the AMA refused to release the report, claiming it mentioned people by name and was potentially libellous. The content of the Arnold report was only revealed when it was eventually tabled in the Northern Territory Legislative Assembly by the then Labor opposition leader Maggie Hickey.

It was time to up the ante and demonstrate against this conspiracy between the AMA, the hospital and the public service. A small group of doctors made a banner that said 'FREE SPEECH?' in letters more than a metre tall. As hospital photographer, I had keys to the roof and it was decided to unfurl the banner from there on a Sunday night. The hospital was eleven storeys high and a Darwin landmark; first thing on Monday morning, the banner would be seen for miles around.

I gave the keys to the others and they put the banner in place. After everyone had come back down from the roof, the lock on the door was superglued to prevent the security staff removing the banner as soon as it was noticed. The next morning it was seen and talked about and photographed, and stayed there until eleven o'clock, when security finally drilled out the locks and got onto the roof to remove it. But it had served its purpose. *Time* magazine published a photograph of the 'FREE SPEECH?' banner and an article that described the underlying issues and the sense of injustice that had provoked it.

What a shitstorm erupted. Suspicion fell on me, because of my battle with the Health Department and my possession of the roof keys. I pleaded ignorance, and had a good alibi. While it was never established who was involved, my keys were confiscated and that was the end of my privileges as hospital photographer. The claim was made that the disabling of the locks meant there was no access to the lift shaft and that if there'd been an emergency in the hospital, hundreds of lives could have been lost.

All this took a toll on me and on my relationship with Tristan, who, not long after, packed up and moved back to Adelaide. This was not the end of our relationship but it was the end of us living together as a couple. As for me, with Reed in charge of NT Health I could foresee another stalled career, just as in the Parks Service. It felt like sweet justice in 1997 when, as deputy chief minister, Reed—who always pushed an anti-gay agenda—was caught out buying pornographic videos, *Highway Hunks* and *Hot Firemen*, from a Sydney sex shop, only to claim they were for the purposes of 'research'.[2]

The hospital bureaucracy and I were never to reconcile, and I had no wish to go back. I decided instead to set up an after-hours general practice—Ausdoc Mobile. At first I had a partner, another doctor, Lynton Stevens, who'd also just left the hospital, but he returned to Adelaide. So I carried on alone setting up the business.

In my new Holden Barina, I took to the streets of Darwin to provide after-hours medical care to anyone who wanted it. It was soon clear that the main consumers of the service would be the city's drug users and sex workers. Territory law made it a crime to prescribe drugs for those addicted, and any medication using opiates had to be for a patient in pain. Drug users who were 'hanging out' when supplies were short or they were broke could not lawfully be helped, and would inject anything they could in desperation. I saw the provision of clean opiates to those addicted as a clear example of harm minimisation and often provided them with methadone syrup.

I also wrote prescriptions for morphine tablets, which would help an addict get through withdrawal, as long as they were prepared to tell me that they were experiencing pain. I later found that some of my prescriptions were being shared, or sold on the black market, and I was told to come in for an interview with the Health Department, that I was prescribing too much morphine. Tristan, who knew more about the system than I did, told me I was getting not a briefing but a warning.

The work took me all over Darwin and the nearby rural area, from family homes with sick kids, to some seedy and fairly dodgy places, like the area down by the wharves. Some of the people on the fishing boats were heavy drug users and

I'd be down there on the boats at midnight with my bag. Although I was carrying drugs with me and was threatened a few times, I never came to physical harm. People sometimes got angry and wanted more than I was prepared to provide, but generally accepted my explanation. I did take precautions. As this was before the days of mobile phones, I relied on a running sheet showing where I was going to be at what time, and I made it clear to the people I was seeing my whereabouts were known. The closest I came to being hurt was when I went into a place in a very poor part of Darwin where there were a lot of drug users and, more dangerously, a lot of drug dealing. A fierce dog, a pit bull, sprang at me. Its chain brought it up just a few inches short of my throat, but its claws ripped my shirt to shreds. I still sweat when I think back about that.

Under Marshall Perron, the Northern Territory government policy on drug use was utterly hypocritical. It basically claimed that there were no local Territory drug addicts, only drug-using visitors from out of state. This meant the Territory didn't have to provide any residential rehabilitation services. In a bizarre policy dreamed up by then Territory Minister for Health, Fred Finch, the government's solution was to put suspected drug users on buses to get them back to their interstate homes. Inevitably, this would have applied to many of my patients. Unbelievably, Finch tried to get this policy passed through the Northern Territory Legislative Assembly and Minister Finch tried to implement it. One of my patients became the first to receive his one-way ticket south but Greyhound refused to take him. I then contacted southern media and explained what was happening.

'You're joking,' the reporter said.

The report went out on *AM*. The story had overtones of what was done in the racist southern states of the US, and an embarrassed Territory government had to abandon the idea.

To get around the restriction on my writing of opiate prescriptions, I set up a video-conference link with Lynton

Stevens, who was now a doctor in Adelaide. That was 1995, long before today's e-consultations. My sample patient explained to Lynton that he was addicted to narcotics. After listening to the story and asking some questions Lynton then faxed us a prescription, something he could legally do in South Australia. It was a stunt to draw attention to the absurdity of the Territory's drug laws. By this time I'd become friendly with Fairfax's Darwin correspondent Gay Alcorn, and a report drawing attention to these drug laws ran nationally in *The Age* and *Sydney Morning Herald*.

I don't know how long I could have gone on in that role as a Darwin after-hours GP. But it didn't matter, as something would happen soon that would change my life forever.

PART II

NINE

First in the world

*Bring the machine around on Sunday afternoon and
I'll die around two.*

Bob Dent, 1996

Max Bell, a taxi driver in Broken Hill, was sixty-seven
years old and had stomach cancer. About two months
before the *Rights of the Terminally Ill Act* was due to be
enacted, and I was still doing my mobile after-hours medical
practice, he contacted me. He was in a very bad way; surgery
on his stomach had left him with constant nausea, vomiting
and an inability to eat solid food and he had heard about my
support for the new euthanasia law in the north. He told me
of his life during one memorable out-of-the-blue phone call.
He asked if the Territory law might work for him and I said I
thought it would; after all, he was terminally ill, with no hope
of recovery. So, I flew down from Darwin to Broken Hill
and met him. With Tristan now back in Adelaide I had been
spending some time in Broken Hill, as she was doing regular
locums there as a paediatrician and I really liked the place.

When I met Max, I saw how very sick he was. We again
discussed the possibility of him using the ROTI law. Now
that he had a glimmer of hope, Max took matters into his
own hands; he had his pet dog put down, put his house up
for sale and drove his cab, under huge duress, to Darwin.

Dying was his intention, but in fact he hadn't quite given up all hope. He had an idea in the back of his mind that the tropical warmth, sunshine and beauty of the Top End might just heal him.

Max was a feisty character. He'd been a pro-golfer, a boxer and a bodyguard and he'd packed his golf clubs and boxing gloves for the trip to Darwin. It irks me that you have no control over the way you are portrayed after death. The stage play *Last Cab to Darwin*, by Reg Cribb and Jeremy Sims, trashes Max's life and reputation. Cribb said that his play was based on the real-life character of Max Bell, but he created a womanising drunk. In the play, I am depicted as a conniving, death-loving doctor. The awful times that Max and I shared didn't deserve this treatment. But then, it's common for dramatists such as Cribb and Sims to be more interested in the effects of their 'art' and their own careers than on any real attempt to understand the truth.[1]

Anyway, the drive north really knocked Max around. He was desperately ill and on his arrival I had him admitted to Darwin Hospital, as I set about getting the necessary signatures of a palliative care specialist, a surgical specialist and a psychiatrist, as the law required. What they had to do was quite simple: a doctor had to certify that Max was dying, that his palliative care options had been explained to him and that he was of sound mind. They didn't have to endorse euthanasia, they just had to certify that this poor bastard was dying, something you could tell at twenty paces. I rang every doctor I could think of but couldn't find a single one in any of the above categories who was willing even to see him. To his credit, Marshall Perron visited Max in hospital, but no doctor would.

The AMA's campaign had put the fear of god into the medical fraternity, whose concern for their own legal safety seemed paramount. Chris Wake, its president, had successfully spread the rumour that doctors could be charged retrospectively if the ROTI Act were overturned. It was clear the issue itself had doctors running scared.

After three weeks, and still very sick, Max had had enough of waiting. He signed himself out of hospital, clambered into his old Commodore taxi and, after staying a night at my place, set off on the 3000-kilometre journey, vomiting his way back to Broken Hill. He was furious with me for not warning him about the pitfalls of his Darwin plan. His parting words were, 'You didn't do your homework, boy.'

There was no way I could leave things that way. I went to Broken Hill a week later and, with some of his friends, helped Max get reasonably comfortable in his house, which we'd managed to get taken off the market. All his possessions had been sold though, so we had to get him a bed and some kitchen items, and looked after him. I had my swag and camped in his lounge room. Nurses from the hospital came and went.

One day he said to me, 'I want you to have the car.'

He knew that I was using Tristan's car, an old Sigma. I said I was fine, but he insisted. I told him he could put this in his will if he wanted to, but he had already filled in the transfer of ownership form. I took it to the Motor Registry and used the car—the Commodore taxi—for the next fifteen years. With its meter still installed in the dashboard, I would often feel Max with me as I drove.

I stayed with Max until he was so weak he had to move into palliative care in Broken Hill Base Hospital. Delirious on morphine and with no control over the process, Max died over a period of three days, in just the way he'd dreaded.

So from Max, there were multiple lessons learnt, about laws, the character of doctors, palliative care and politics. But another lesson was more positive. Earlier on, Murray McLaughlin, a journalist on the ABC's *Four Corners* program, had asked me if I knew anyone intending to use the Territory Act. I put him in touch with Max, and *Four Corners* went to

Katherine, to film Max as he arrived and on his drive north, and later in Darwin. The result was a powerful *Four Corners* program entitled 'The Road to Nowhere', which revealed Max's terrible suffering and went to air just as he was making his return trip.[2]

The day after the program screened, a surgeon called Jon Wardill rang me. He had been one of the many doctors who had refused to see Max and sign his papers.

'I've just seen *Four Corners*, about your patient.'

'Yes,' I said.

'I felt like shit,' he said.

'Yeah, well …'

'If it ever happens again, ring me.'

Wardill's reaction was a shock and emphasised to me the power of the image. Journalist Gay Alcorn had written some powerful stories about Max and his time in Darwin for *The Age* newspaper, but it was the live action on the television screen that hit home. If this taught me one thing, it was never to underestimate the impact of television in portraying a human story to change opinions.

★ ★ ★

Jon Wardill got his chance sooner than he might have expected.

Bob Dent, a Darwin resident, was a carpenter, a fiercely independent character, whose life had been reduced to what he called 'a rollercoaster of pain' by five years of prostate cancer and its treatment. Bob saw the ROTI Act as a gift—a way to end his suffering and die with dignity, with those who cared for him. He contacted me and asked for my help.

By this time my interest in voluntary euthanasia was such that I had read much about the subject, and had learned about American doctor Jack Kevorkian's involvement in assisted suicide, in particular the machines he invented to help people die. His first was the 'Thanatron', a mechanical device consisting of three bottles suspended from a metal frame for dispensing lethal drugs, via an intravenous drip, into a patient's vein. Kevorkian's other machine of note was the 'Mercitron' (or mercy machine), which was a gas mask connected to a canister of carbon monoxide. Both devices provided in-built patient control in the act of dying, something I agreed with. I had decided to see if I could improve on Kevorkian's machines.

With the help of Des Carne, my friend from the days in the Sydney squat, I had built what I called the 'Deliverance Machine'.[3] It consisted of a laptop computer that automated the delivery of the drugs through a line to a venous cannula. The person who wanted to die had to answer three questions that appeared on the laptop screen:

1 Are you aware that if you go ahead to the last screen and press the 'Yes' button, you will be given a lethal dose of medications and die?;
2 Are you certain you understand that if you proceed and press the 'Yes' button on the next screen that you will die?;
3 In 15 seconds you will be given a lethal injection ... press 'Yes' to proceed.

If the wrong button were pressed, or a button pressed outside of a specified time limit, the program would stop and need to be restarted.

This was, in effect, doctor-assisted suicide, as opposed to voluntary euthanasia, and it had the great advantage of allowing the doctor to step aside, leaving the patient in complete control of the process. It also took the doctor out of the patient's personal space and allowed them free access to their loved ones. Bob Dent saw it as the answer to his problem. But there was still the question of getting doctors' signatures in order to comply with the law. I remembered Jon Wardill's pledge and rang him.

'Now's your chance,' I said.

His reply was crisp. 'Bring him in.'

Even with a leading surgeon's signature secured, it wasn't easy to get the others we needed to complete the requirements. I rang practically every psychiatrist in Australia. Among the myriad excuses I heard were, 'I agree with you but I simply can't because I'm pregnant', or 'I want to help, but my wife won't let me.'

A colleague suggested I ring John Ellard, a Sydney psychiatrist. I hesitated to do this, remembering him from Sydney medical school days, where he was a formidable presence. But in desperation, I did eventually ring, and Professor Ellard immediately said he'd fly to Darwin and see Bob.

'What about the College of Psychiatrists?' I asked, wondering how he'd deal with his peers.

'*I am the college*,' was his simple reply. In August 1996 Professor Ellard travelled to Darwin, saw Bob and signed the necessary papers.

Finally, I could tell Bob that everything was in order. He was a Buddhist, and he'd been to the Darwin temple to say his farewells and give his thanks. He said, 'Bring the machine around on Sunday afternoon and I'll die around two.' Then he added, 'Come to lunch.'

On Sunday morning I packed up the equipment (I'd tested it more times than I could count), and drove to the suburb of Tiwi, where Bob and his wife Judy lived. I've described the lunch in some detail in many a media interview, including on Andrew Denton's *Enough Rope* program on ABC television in 2008.[4]

The lunch, which took about an hour, was something of an ordeal, though I was the most agitated person there. We ate ham sandwiches and drank stout and, as I told Denton, my mouth was like sand. I almost choked on my sandwich and had only the smallest sip of stout, just enough to keep my mouth wet so I could speak. While it's hot in Darwin in September, it's not as hot as it gets; yet I remember my shirt was drenched in sweat. Conversation was difficult, as it is when a person is about to die. I felt I had to watch every word I said; I tried hard not to reference the future because, for Bob, there wasn't one. We watched an AFL game on TV, and then Bob left the room and laid down on the lounge on the veranda.

To say I was nervous as I prepared the machine would be an understatement. Surprisingly, the needle of the cannula slid easily into Bob's vein the first try. That doesn't always happen and I'd been worried there might be a problem. I then connected up the syringe of lethal barbiturates and booted up the computer, and stepped away.

'Are you sure, Bob?' I said.

His answer was to lean towards the computer and press the button that asked the first question about the process. He then pressed the button again, and again for the last time. As the fifteen seconds it took for the delivery of the drugs ticked away, I realised that my shirt was dripping with sweat.

I had two thoughts: I was glad that Bob was getting the peaceful death he wanted but I was also acutely aware that this was the first time something like this had ever happened. And, as I watched from the other side of the room, I knew that nothing would ever be quite the same again.

Bob sighed as his wife held him and he fell into a deep sleep. With her still holding him, he died in just a few minutes. We sat there, still and silent, for about half an hour. Slowly, she lifted her hand in a gesture, and I came over and confirmed that Bob was dead.

I must have removed the cannula and packed up the machine, but I have no clear memory of doing so. Then I left. I had a book of death-certificate forms and I signed one for Bob. The regulations to the Act stipulated that the cause of death be entered as the underlying disease; the legislation recognised that people didn't want 'suicide' on their death certificates. In Bob's case, I simply entered 'prostate cancer', accompanied by 'respiratory arrest', which is an accurate description of the effect of the administered Nembutal and Pancuroniun, although the drugs didn't get a mention.

Outside, I took a deep breath and slowly drove home. There was a suspicion in Darwin that the law may have been used and I started to get phone calls from the media, asking me to confirm or deny the rumours. I wanted some time. Judy Dent was shaky and not ready for the media frenzy that we knew would follow, and wanted to wait. I went along with this and was pleased to have some time to calm down and collect my thoughts. I remember getting a call from Kerry O'Brien, of the ABC's *7.30 Report*.

He said, 'I know the law's been used. Will you talk about it?'

I said, 'No.'

'Are you saying the law hasn't been used?'

'That's right,' I lied.

O'Brien has never forgiven me for that. A similar situation developed much later after the death of Norma Hall, adventurer Lincoln Hall's mother, at which I was present. This matter is covered in *Killing Me Softly*, but what is not mentioned there is that it almost cost me a friendship.

In 2000, Norma was terminally ill with lung cancer and wanting to die. After failing to get the palliative-care doctors to agree to what amounted to slow euthanasia (terminal sedation), for which she had my support, she stopped eating and drinking. She then ingested the entire contents of a bottle of liquid morphine that had been prescribed for her. My journalist friend at the ABC, Murray McLaughlin, then working for *7.30 Report*, had followed Norma's case closely, and had filmed her handing an open letter, declaring her intention, to Peter Baume, a former Federal Health Minister.

Murray considered he had the right to be kept fully informed of the progress of the case, but I found myself lying to him about exactly when Norma died. Her death was not easy. The liquid morphine she drank did not kill her immediately, and it took many hours for her to die. If the news of her death had got out on the Friday it occurred, it would have dominated the media over the weekend, to her children's distress. There was also the matter of the law and my exact role in her death. My own actions are often under the police spotlight, a worry that few journalists have.

My lie to Murray meant that it was Monday before the story broke. He felt betrayed. Our friendship cooled and has only recently come anywhere near recovering. I didn't regret what I'd done but, to this day, I feel conflicted about giving the media what they want while trying to consider the feelings and emotions of those close at hand, of those good people whose lives and deaths are playing out.

The documents relating to Bob Dent's case—the death certificate and the certificates signed by the three doctors— were lodged with the coroner on the Wednesday, which was when everything became public. So, I bought forty-eight hours by lying to Kerry O'Brien, and others. I was gutted and close to tears at the press conference after Bob's death. Nothing could have prepared me for the global publicity that followed. From that moment on, I was typecast—by my supporters, as a determined advocate for the right to choose; by my opponents, as 'Dr Death'. Three more of my patients— Janet Mills, Valerie Purcell and Bill Worthington—all used the Deliverance Machine over the following months to die peacefully, and at the time and place of their choosing.

Janet Mills' case presented a particular problem. She was from Naracoorte in South Australia, and was suffering from mycosis fungoides, a rare skin cancer that breaks down the skin cells, leaving scarring, recurrent infection and constant, unendurable itching. This is the disease that killed Paul Eddington—Jim Hacker of the BBC's *Yes Minister* and *Yes, Prime Minister* television series. Janet, with her husband, Dave— a shearer and one of the nicest and strongest people you'd ever hope to meet—came to Darwin to take advantage of the law. Over the years, Janet had been given every available treatment and she'd had enough.

Janet was shockingly ill when I visited her at her motel in Darwin; the room smelled of what was effectively her festering body. She was admitted to Darwin Private Hospital and given a palliative care bed, while I ran around trying again to get the necessary signatures organised for her. The problem was that we needed a Territory-registered specialist to sign the papers and confirm diagnosis, but I couldn't find one. An Adelaide dermatologist with the unforgettable name of Jack Russell had testified to Janet's terminal condition, but that wouldn't do, as he was down south.

I organised a media conference for Janet and Dave to appeal for a Territory specialist to come forward and help them. Her courage in facing the world, in her wasted, disfigured condition, was extraordinary. The hospital wouldn't cooperate, so the press conference was held at Bob Dent's house. But the appeal didn't work. No doctor put up their hand.

I became very despondent, and one night while sitting with Dave, having a few beers, I said I didn't think we were going to be able to do it. He wouldn't have it.

'We've come all this way,' he said, 'and she's so very sick. You can't give up now.'

Tristan even tried the doctors in her field of paediatrics, only to get short shrift with comments like, 'What's mycosis fungoides got to do with paediatrics?' I rang every specialist in the Territory; it didn't matter what their field was, they only had to be a specialist and undertake a normal consultation with the patient.[5] As I worked my way down the list of more than sixty names, I developed a sort of patter:

'Hello, this is Philip Nitschke. I'm trying to find a specialist to see a patient of mine who's dying of mycosis fungoides and I need ...'

The response was almost exactly the same every time. Something like, 'Give me a break. I'm not a dermatologist.'

I'd say, 'Thank you very much,' and ring off, then dial again. Eventually, I reached the orthopaedic specialists and started by ringing Steve Baddeley, the sports-car-driving surgeon who had fixed my heel years earlier and later supervised my first intern term. I gave him my spiel and was about to hang up when he interrupted me.

'I'll do it,' he said. 'I'll see her.'

I could hardly believe my ears and kept on talking until his response sank in.

'Did you hear me? I believe in what you're doing,' he said.

Dave cried when I told him. We bundled up Janet and took her to Steve Baddeley's rooms in the Darwin CBD and he gave her a meticulous examination. He'd been in touch with the Adelaide dermatologist, and had researched the disease and Janet's condition. He signed the papers. Ever since, Steve has copped flak over his actions from people who say he acted wrongly, that an orthopaedic specialist should not be signing the papers of a person dying from a dermatological condition. Those who criticised him have misread the Act; all the Act stipulated was that a 'normal consultation' had to be conducted with a specialist. Adelaide dermatologist Dr Warren Weightman, a right-to-life stalwart, compounded the confusion when he weighed in with his opinion that mycosis fungoides wasn't even a terminal disease. To his great credit, Steve stood his ground and remains a strong supporter of voluntary euthanasia.

Janet Mills had paid her dues. For years, when hospitalised, she'd made it possible for doctors and medical students to see her and learn about this dreadful condition. If anyone had earned the right to a peaceful death, she had. And she got it. She died in Dave's arms.

★ ★ ★

The question I am most commonly asked about when describing these events is, 'How did you feel when you killed these patients?'

The answer has several aspects. First, it was paramount I hold myself together. After the deaths, I was always in a mess, but saw no point in letting the patient's family see this. So, I managed to keep my composure, but it was always difficult. Knowing someone is going to die at a certain time puts you in a unique and very strange place. On those four occasions, travelling to meet with a patient who would die before I left, gave me a strange and uncomfortable feeling, similar I imagine to one that executioners must experience.

In *The Australian Book of Atheism*, which was published in 2011, I tried to describe the effect of these deaths on me. I wrote: '… each time, as I packed up the machine and walked back into the sunlight, it felt good to be alive and good to have done the right thing. And as for any possible breach of "god's law"? What god, and what law would that be?' But there was more to this than meets the eye.

When you are personally involved in the act of killing a person—even if it is what they want, and even if it is lawful—in my experience the action has a strange effect on you. In my case, it created a desperate need for something life-affirming. It was as though I needed to prove to myself that it was not me who had just passed on. It was not me who, in Jean Paul Sartre's words, had entered the existential nothingness, which is how an atheist like me sees the state of being deceased, of being dead. I'm in agreement with Kerry Packer on this one: 'let me tell you, son, there's fucking nothing there'. I've been with plenty of people when they have died, but it was the act of being instrumental in these peoples death that made these deaths so different.

So when these four patients died, my response was a desperate craving for intimacy. In retrospect I think I needed to feel a connection to those still living and to the world as a whole as it continued to turn. At the time I was having an affair with a local journalist in Darwin. She—we— came together in a manner not dissimilar to Bob Seger's 'Nightmoves' song in which we both got what we wanted, using each other as we went. I can now fully understand where David Walsh is heading with his MONA Museum's Sex and Death theme. There is something primordial about the beginning and ending of life. I'm pleased that a replica of my Deliverance Machine has found a spot to be exhib- ited within a context that asks important social, political and artistic questions of the two.

Apart from the four people who used the ROTI law to die, there was a fifth, Esther Wild. Esther had been a nurse at Royal Darwin Hospital and was terminally ill with carcinoid syndrome, a rare type of cancer. Esther qualified to make use of the law but was prevented from doing so for reasons that should shame the people involved, as I will explain later. Now though, even as these initial four people used the ROTI Act to put an end to their suffering, opponents of the Territory legislation were mustering force to move against me and every Australian citizen who believed in their right to voluntary euthanasia.

TEN

The overturn

*There is nothing moral about our exercising a free
conscience vote as members of parliament and then
voting to deny to others the right to exercise their
conscience. What possible right do[es] Kevin Andrews ...
have to have exercised Bob Dent's conscience for him?*

Anthony Albanese, Australian House of
Representatives, *Speech, Second Reading
Euthanasia Laws Bill 1996*

I don't remember when I first heard the name Kevin Andrews,
but it has been stuck in my mind ever since.

Kevin James Andrews is a pro-life lawyer from Gippsland,
in country Victoria. A devout Catholic, he entered Parliament
in 1991, and by 1995 was a backbencher in John Howard's
newly elected conservative government. As one of the four
founders of the Lyons Forum, a secretive, ultra-conservative
faction within the Liberal Party, Andrews is about as reactionary and doggedly religious as Australian politicians get. He is
credited, if that's the word, with naming the group after that
historical anachronism Dame Enid Lyons. The forum was
very influential under Howard, as it set itself to work against
progressive moves in such areas as abortion, cloning and stem-
cell research. Euthanasia was, obviously, a prime target.

In contrast to the former prime minister, Paul Keating, who had declared the ROTI Act 'within power' and therefore not a matter for 'disallowance' (overturning) or meddling by the federal government, John Howard stated his opposition to ROTI less than four months after he was elected. On 25 June 1996, he floated the idea of a Private Member's Bill to block the law. Two days later, Andrews stepped forward to do Howard's bidding, announcing that he would introduce precisely such a Bill. Howard was said to have conspired with Andrews to introduce his Private Member's Bill, indicating that the government would offer support if the matter came before the High Court.

When word of Andrews' manoeuvrings reached me in Darwin, I feared the worst. I knew the Howard government's agenda was solidly right wing—Howard had proudly declared himself the most conservative Liberal Party leader since Menzies—and I was very aware that the Federal Parliament was awash with the religious, on both sides of the chamber. The then opposition leader, Kim Beazley, joined Howard in making his opposition to voluntary euthanasia clear early on.

In 1996, with ROTI in force but under attack, I was fighting on multiple fronts—trying to helping patients meet the requirements of the legislation and trying to organise support to defend the law itself. I was living a rather fragile hand-to-mouth existence, bulk-billing some of the patients who were still on my books, and being stretched thin financially.

I took it upon myself to try to organise a national defence of the ROTI Act—collective action. Several states had state voluntary euthanasia societies and I hoped to focus them on this cause. I travelled around the country to meet representatives of these groups and managed to set up a strategy meeting to bring these miniature fiefdoms together.

I was dismayed when I found that there was no great enthusiasm for a collective stance. The Voluntary Euthanasia

Society of Victoria was a standout. The president of this organisation, Dr Rodney Syme, and the secretary, Kay Koetsier,
were taking a completely different, state-focused, tack. The
Victorians would not support any campaign to lobby federal
politicians, arguing that if the Andrews Bill passed there would
be a national outcry. They were adamant that at that point, Jeff
Kennett, the Victorian Premier and an ardent states-righter,
would pass voluntary euthanasia legislation and thumb his
nose at the Federal Parliament. I thought this politically naïve
and thought as Dale Kerrigan of *The Castle* would have said,
'*Tell 'em they're dreamin'*.'

In allowing a free vote on Kevin Andrews' Euthanasia
Laws Bill 1996, John Howard knew he was on safe ground.
Although a clear majority of ordinary Australians believed
that a voluntary euthanasia law was desirable, the opponents
were politically, financially and organisationally powerful, and
had little opposition from a voluntary euthanasia movement
that had failed to unite.

What became known as the 'Euthanasia No' campaign
was spearheaded by sub-committees and individuals with
church backing. Its ringleaders included Gillard government
minister Tony Burke, then a shadow cabinet member; wealthy
investment banker James Dominguez CBE AM, who has
since been awarded the quaintly termed papal honour
'Knight Commander of the Order of St Gregory the Great';
and Paul Kelly, then editor-in-chief—now 'editor-at-large'—
of *The Australian* newspaper. In his influential role as an issue-
presenter and opinion-maker, Kelly was (and is) an unabashed
opponent of end-of-life choice.

Although there were Liberals, like Amanda Vanstone
and Petro Georgiou, who supported voluntary euthanasia,
the majority on the government side were in the Andrews
camp. Greens leader Bob Brown and Labor members such
as Jenny Macklin, Simon Crean and Anthony Albanese[1] were

outspoken defenders of ROTI, but many others in the Labor Opposition were very willing to see it overturned.

Although the Northern Territory had the right to draft such a law, and set the conditions for the ROTI Act to be passed, the Territory Parliament had a crucial vulnerability. While it is an historical quirk, section 122 of the Australian Constitution allows for the Federal Parliament to also make laws for the Territories of the nation (for example, the Northern Territory, the ACT and Norfolk Island). By definition, this same section allows the Federal Parliament to make a law preventing a Territory from making another law. That is what the Andrews Bill set out to do.

People queuing to use ROTI— Bob Dent, in particular— were acutely aware of this threat and often raised it with me. In September 1996, shortly before he died, Bob dictated a letter to be sent to the members of the Federal Parliament. He explained his condition and why he had decided to end his life. He continued, 'I read with increasing horror newspaper stories of Kevin Andrews's attempts to overturn the most compassionate piece of legislation in the world. (Actually, my wife has to read the newspaper stories to me because I can no longer focus my eyes.)' Then Bob hit the nail on the head. 'If you don't want to use voluntary euthanasia, then don't do it, but don't deny me the right to use it if I want to.'

The politicking went on and I remember an amusing incident when it looked like the Andrews Bill would reach the Senate. The Senate decided to send a committee of inquiry around the country, with a bunch of them turning up in Darwin to look into the question of whether the Federal Government should intervene to remove the Territory legislation. The hearings were convened, and the public invited to come in and put their views to the committee of assembled senators. The thing that stuck in my mind was this chap who had come in from the Victoria River region, and who looked like he'd been riding his horse for three days. He was bushman through and through, with his moleskins, Akubra hat and sun-wrinkled face. After he'd been sitting quietly up the back for a while, it was finally his turn to speak. He slowly got up and said, 'I can't understand why youse senators are so keen to try and get rid of our Territory law on euthanasia. Because, from what I can see, most of us Territorians want this law.' He continued, 'I think it's about eighty per cent of us Territorians who want this law and I think that oughta just about constitute a mandate! In fact, I think it's the sorta mandate that oughta give youse politicians an orgasm!'

Everybody started laughing. Brian Harradine, the Catholic hardliner, seemed to wake up briefly. All the cowboy had done was state the obvious—if eighty per cent of people want something that does not infringe the rights of the other twenty per cent, why the hell would you be so keen to take it away from them?

In the campaigning, and prolonged and vigorous debate in both houses of Parliament, every conceivable argument for and against voluntary euthanasia was raised. The persistently irritating South Australian MP Christopher Pyne (himself a practising Catholic) trotted out the church's line to the letter, citing Armageddon in the Netherlands because of their euthanasia-decriminalisation experiment. The Dutch had decriminalised doctor-assisted suicide in 1993 and this allowed doctors who followed the guidelines to help a sick patient without being prosecuted, even though the act was still considered illegal. Full legalisation of the practice did not occur in that country till 2002. At this stage though, rumours and myths about the dangerous practices going on in Holland were circulating, and Pyne trotted them all out as fact. He ended his speech in Parliament with the rather ill-thought-out conclusion that the passing of the Andrews Bill would some-how save lives: 'I cannot in all good conscience oppose a Bill that I know, if passed, will save the lives of Australian people.'[2]

More disappointing, perhaps because it was unexpected, was the attitude of ALP heavyweight Barry Jones, who said he was 'singularly unimpressed by the argument that, [just] because public opinion polls support euthanasia, the Northern Territory's law should be allowed to stand'. Speaking in the ROTI Act's defence, Bob Brown kept it simple, referring back to the words of Wes Lanhupuy, the Northern Territory MP who had cast the winning vote for the original legislation, back in Darwin in 1995. The former member for Arnhem said:

> After all the debate and controversy, I said to people that I hoped that they would be able to give me the right to exercise my right as an individual. It is not hard to ask for a person's rights as an individual. A man lives his life, whether for or against the law, and irrespective of whether he has received the rights that he has demanded or has had a cheerful life or otherwise. When he is about to make his last request, should we be in a position to deny him that last right which he wants? That is the question which I believe honourable members of this House will have to come to grips with by themselves ...

Brown continued:

> With no less charge, we in this Senate are challenged to give people that right, and not to deny it to them. We are charged to have the courage of the Northern Territory legislators. We are charged to respond to the undeniable force of public opinion in this country, and I charge all senators who have not yet made up their minds in this matter to think carefully about that preponderant public opinion—to give the people a say if you cannot make a decision against overriding this legislation, which will set the clock back decades in

what is an inexorable move in the global community
as well as here in Australia towards granting everybody
the right to opt for voluntary euthanasia.

The Andrews Bill was finally passed by a handful of votes
in the Senate, and now only needed the Royal Assent of the
governor-general to become law. At that point, I decided to
take a leaf out of the Vietnam draft-resisters' book.

I had watched the debate on the television in Bob
Brown's Parliament House office and saw that it was obvious
the bill would pass. I mentioned to Natasha, one of Bob's
legal researchers, that I thought it would make a good point
to burn copies of the ROTI Act and the Northern Territory
Constitution on the steps of Parliament House, and she
organised photocopies from the parliamentary library. The
ROTI Act only amounted to six pages, but the Territory
Constitution was a thick stack of paper. You can't just drop
a match on a bundle of paper like that on a cold windy
Canberra night and expect it to burn; you need an accelerant.

'We need some petrol,' I said, 'but how do you get that in
Parliament House?

She said, 'Leave it to me.'

Because she had a staff pass and didn't have to go through
the regular security, she was able to smuggle in a small screw-
top petrol bottle. Handbags are marvellous things at times.
When Bob Brown and I, and others, were ready to walk out
to face the nation's media, I excused myself for a minute, took
the papers into a toilet and soaked them in the petrol. Out on
the steps, in front of the cameras, I lit a match and they went
up in a sheet of flame. It made a dramatic newspaper photo.

★ ★ ★

The most immediate victim of the Andrews Bill was
Esther Wild. In my book *Killing Me Softly*, I wrote at length

of Esther's terrible plight. Anyone interested in the intersection of morality and politics, and the hazards of providing slow euthanasia by morphine infusion, should read that account. What Esther had to endure is painful to recall. Here, I'd like simply to put on the record the cruelty of those politicians who resisted her wish to be allowed to die peacefully under the ROTI Act. Esther had already qualified as someone who could use the law; she had her papers signed and was ready. However, she didn't want to die right away; an avid gardener, she wanted to see the flowers in her large tropical garden bloom one more time. In qualifying to use the law, she had her insurance policy of choice in place. Or so she thought.

Once the Andrews Bill passed the Senate, the timing of Esther's death came down to the governor-general, Sir William Deane. She knew she would need to act before the ROTI law was lost, and decided on the Easter holiday period as her time to die. However, Deane would have none of it, taking the extraordinary step of giving assent to the Andrews legislation late on the Thursday afternoon before Good Friday. In doing so, he ignored a personal plea from Esther to wait at least until after the Easter public holiday.

Deane's reputation is forever tarnished—in my estimation —by his actions, and that he then delegated to his press secretary the job of telling Esther of his decision, behaviour I felt was nothing short of pathetic.

And so Esther was left with no choice but to die a slow and difficult death. I gradually increased Esther's morphine dose, but even in doing this there was risk in this post-ROTI environment. Again, Steve Baddeley came to my assistance, by driving his Porsche out to Esther's house in the rural outskirts of Darwin and providing his support for this grim slow euthanasia procedure. At one point Esther briefly regained consciousness, and called out to her close friend Cathy who was nearby. Her final words, 'Am I dead yet, Cathy?'

Murray McLaughlin made another *Four Corners* program, this time about Esther, called 'The Dying Game', and there was a subsequent medical inquiry into what actually had happened.[3] Steve Baddeley backed me all the way.

Some time after Esther's death, her partner, Martin Williams, confronted Deane on one of the governor-general's visits to Darwin. Martin pushed through the crowd outside the city's art gallery and yelled, 'You bastard, you're the one who didn't have the guts to let my Esther have a decent death.'

ELEVEN

Moving on

*May I wish Mr Kevin Andrews a long and
excruciatingly painful life.*

Letter to the editor, *Sydney Morning Herald*

E ven though I had become the face of the voluntary
euthanasia struggle, I still wasn't consciously intending to
make this my life's work. That crept up on me.

After the disappointment of failing to organise a united
national euthanasia movement, I changed tactics. In forming
the Voluntary Euthanasia Research Foundation (VERF),
now called Exit International, my idea was to provide people
with information about their end-of-life options. Sick people
still wanted to die, but I was also being approached by well
people—particularly the elderly—who wanted to know
more about voluntary euthanasia, and in particular, what possibilities now existed with the loss of the ROTI Act. These
people drove the agenda and influenced what happened next;
their needs abolished any thoughts I had about stepping away
from the issue.

VERF wasn't well organised, structurally or financially,
but donations started coming in; one five-figure cash amount
even arrived in a shoebox. I continued to work as a doctor but
I also began to conduct information workshops. The very first
workshop I ran was in Melbourne in 1997. The manager of

the Downtowner Motel in Lygon Street, Carlton, Tim Nicholson, had been in Darwin when the voluntary-euthanasia debate raged. He was a strong supporter of the movement, and he provided me with free accommodation and a meeting room to conduct the workshop. I was nervous, although there were no more than a dozen or so elderly people present, sitting around a table. In two ways that first workshop set the pattern of things to come: first, those attending were elderly, average age around seventy-five years, with slightly more women than men and, second, the group wanted to know all they could about how to get the best end-of-life drug, the barbiturate Nembutal. I ran that session in the way that has become standard. I gave a talk outlining practical options, alongside the legal constraints and considerations. I then threw the session open to questions and discussion, saying, 'You tell me what you want to know and I'll do my best to answer.' It was a very small beginning for something that would become bigger than I ever imagined. These days, with Exit workshops running around the world, it's not uncommon to get over two hundred people at such events.

The workshops start with a free public meeting in which I explain to the group why it makes sense for them all to learn how, and acquire the means, to be able to peacefully and reliably end their life at the time of their choosing. It is a simple argument. With no euthanasia legislation in place, no one can lawfully help you die and the penalties for assisting someone are savage. Suicide, though, is not a crime, so if you carry out the act yourself no legal risks are taken. Plan ahead, I argue. Don't leave it until you find yourself so sick and incapable that you have to ask those you love to assist you to get you the lethal drugs you need. This argument strikes a chord, and most of those attending stay on for the following closed workshop, which is the practical Q&A session on how to suicide. To stay on, participants need to join Exit, and that is how much of the funding for the organisation is obtained.

Before VERF, an incorporated association, became Exit International, a public non-profit company with externally audited and publicly viewable accounts, things were very informal. Back then, I was helped by Des Carne, who'd found the Camperdown squat while I was at medical school and helped me build the Deliverance Machine. He came to Darwin, put a demountable on my rural block and started helping set things up. He was self-taught and interested in computers, and created a database so we could coordinate the growing number of letters and email coming in, and also keep an eye on the finances. It was an amateurish outfit though, and our record keeping was fragile.

Since that time, I have been able to eke out a humble financial existence thanks to the generosity and contributions of supporters. While my opponents often accuse me of growing rich out of death, the truth is very different. For the last decade, I have drawn around $50 000 a year as my salary from Exit International, a fraction of what I was making annually when working as a Darwin doctor in the late 1990s. These days, the organisation's main income is from annual memberships and book and merchandise sales, and grosses around $500 000 a year. The average membership age is seventy-five years, and unless there is a good reason, only those over fifty years can join. There are many, though, with good reasons. One memorable example was the Melbourne writer Angelique Flowers, who died in tragic circumstances in September 2008, aged thirty-one. She suffered her whole short life with Crohn's disease, but it wasn't until she received the even worse diagnosis of terminal bowel cancer that she made contact with Exit. We met and talked at length about her options. Shortly after this she acquired the Nembutal she desperately wanted, but was then hospitalised before she was able to use the drug. Her filmed

YouTube appeal to the prime minister at the time, Kevin Rudd, to change the euthanasia laws in Australia has become an important motivator for younger people looking at the euthanasia issue.[1]

In the late 1990s it became clear there was a significant lack of coordination and communication between me, so often on the move, and our Darwin office, creating a number of dangerous situations. A crisis point was reached one day, when I received an agitated and desperate phone call in Sydney from a woman whose ill husband had just killed himself. She kept threatening to go the police, saying that Exit had told her husband to do this, and provided advice, yet I knew nothing about it. As it happened, he'd been in touch with the Darwin office but the information hadn't been passed on to me. Our database just wasn't capable of providing instant access within the organisation to details of every important contact. This crisis passed, and the police were never involved, but it showed me that there was a desperate need for Exit to make use of much better technology.

Today, our records are not only encrypted, but database information is instantly available to all of the organisation's small staff. The system is maintained for us by a professional company on a pro-bono basis. Their incredible work has saved us, so many times, from walking into trouble.[2] It has been quite humbling that such expertise has been provided in this way.

★ ★ ★

In 1998, I relaunched my political career, standing as a candidate against Kevin Andrews in the Melbourne seat of Menzies. This time I worked closely with the Voluntary Euthanasia Society of Victoria, which had so disappointed me when we were trying to defend the Northern Territory legislation. In this campaign, though, they gave me their full support. The

$120 000 in donations stood as a record for funds raised for an independent candidate and showed the level of community support for voluntary euthanasia.

On polling day, I received over 10 per cent of the primary vote. Many people who had previously voted for Kevin Andrews shifted their vote to me, and for the first time, Andrews failed to obtain an absolute majority. Preferences had to be counted. While the Liberal Party ultimately held the seat (it had previously been considered a safe blue-ribbon seat) no one expected this result. During the campaign, I met Kevin Andrews for the first time at a debate held in a Doncaster hall. We were sitting quite close to each other and exchanged a few civil words, but photographs taken at the time say it all. We were never going to be mates. The 1998 election result must have shocked him. But to my supporters and me, it felt like some small payback for the misery his Andrews Act had caused.

By the new decade, Exit International was up and running, and I was experiencing life on the road. I was travelling extensively both in Australia and overseas, giving workshops, seeing patients, giving talks at conferences and engaging in debates. However, it was not until I met Fiona Stewart in 2001 that my life turned another corner, and with it, Exit's entire modus operandi. Back then, Fiona, a sociologist, was regularly writing opinion columns for *The Australian*, *The Age* and *Herald Sun* newspapers, and was an emerging face of Generation X feminism. She had also recently founded a dot com start-up, the consumer complaints website NotGoodEnough.org.

We met at Brisbane's inaugural Festival of Ideas, at the Powerhouse, on the banks of the Brisbane River. At the time, I was still partnered with Tristan, and Fiona had been in a ten-year relationship with a Melbourne man, Michael. We were introduced at a planning meeting that was held shortly before we took to the stage for a debate titled 'There's no such thing as a new idea'. We were on opposing sides of the podium, with Phillip Adams as chair, and the event was broadcast live-to-air on *Late Night Live* on Radio National. By the end of the debate, Fiona and Lynne Spender (one of my team members) had changed sides, as neither agreed with the line their team was running. That night, Fiona and I started talking, progressing to the bar for a beer, and onwards throughout the rest of the festival. Now, more than a decade on, we haven't stopped.

Our relationship had a difficult beginning. I hesitated, refusing to tell Tristan what was happening. We had been in trouble for some time, mostly because she really wanted to have children and felt that time was running out. I had never had fatherhood ambitions though, and did all I could to avoid talking about the issue. She was hurt and disappointed and felt betrayed; this was the issue that finally drove us apart.

Fiona is much more like me. She is feisty, outspoken and quite radical in her politics, although something of an extrovert, which contrasts with my shyness. On the night we met, Fiona was upfront about her lack of desire to have children. Dogs, yes, she said, kids, no. Indeed, *60 Minutes* had just screened a story in which she featured as an example of a thirty-something professional woman who saw no need to reproduce in order to have a full and rewarding life. In August 2001, Fiona was living in inner Melbourne and, for the next eighteen months, that city was to draw me back time and time again. But it wasn't easy. She came to Darwin for the first time late in 2001, but I wasn't there to meet her. I was in London, trying (with a *60 Minutes* crew) to get to meet Diane Pretty, a motor-neurone-disease sufferer who at that stage was the public face of the campaign for vol- untary euthanasia in Britain. When I finally did get back to Darwin, Fiona came out to my rural shed, and this didn't help at all. After all, she was from Melbourne's South Yarra, and my place in Coolalinga was, well, pretty rough. Despite our fierce attraction, I wondered then and there if Fiona's and my relationship could ever work.

I took her bush, to see a different part of the Territory and to meet different people, in the hope that things between us would improve. Given her politics, I thought she'd be interested in Wave Hill and its history in the struggle for Aboriginal land rights, so we packed our camping gear and set off.

It's about 300 kilometres from Darwin, south to Katherine, and then another 500 kilometres southwest to Wave Hill. The road is sealed all the way, the legacy of the Territory beef industry, but it is a narrow, one-lane bitumen strip. From Katherine we pushed on to the isolated Top Springs pub, halfway between Katherine and Wave Hill. Stuck out in the middle of a mulga flat, it was a notorious bush pub, the one where I'd had my fight with David Quinn all those years ago.

On that first trip we camped out, a short distance from the Dagaragu community. The place had changed enormously from when I was last there; the shed Jenny and I had lived in was long gone. There was a plaque to show where the famous shelter—the one that appears in all the photographs of the Wave Hill strike in the 1970s, including the ones with Frank Hardy, with the Gurindji sign over the heads of the people—used to be, and there was a small museum erected with some of the early photographs and other memorabilia of those days.

Only a handful of the Gurindji people I'd known were still there but Mick (Hoppy Mick) Rangiari was, and we talked with him. He'd been one of the youngest of the original strikers, and the last one left. The conditions seemed as grim as they'd always been, and there were people sitting around in the dirt with their dogs, in much the same way as they had back in 1973. I wondered what Fiona would make of it all.

I needn't have worried. She coped with everything, including the humidity and the heat—and the January monsoon thunderstorms. Our mosquito net saved us from a fate worse than death. The trip was a great success and Fiona fell for the Territory and, thankfully, for me.

She agreed to give Darwin a full-time go in early 2003. More than a decade on, she is my best friend and my lover, my sounding board, and my staunchest and most loyal confidant. I would be lost without her. Our impromptu wedding at the Stained Glass Chapel in Las Vegas, on 17 November 2009, was the best day of my life.

TWELVE

The courage of Caren Jenning

I am going to end my life. I am not going to die in gaol.

Caren Jenning to the author, September 2008

In 2005, Caren Jenning was seventy-five years of age and in remission from breast cancer. She was a long-time Exit member and the informal coordinator of our Sydney chapter. Over the years, Caren often mentioned that she had various friends who wanted information about end of life drugs. While some of them joined Exit and came to workshops for this purpose, Caren's friend of forty years, Graeme Wylie, a retired Qantas pilot who had been diagnosed with Alzheimer's disease, said he had no time for this 'Exit Club', as he called it. However, by late 2005, Graeme's health problems were spiralling out of control. He told those around him that he wanted to end it before he got to the stage where he couldn't 'wipe his bum or recognise Shirley', his partner of more than two decades. Caren contacted me and said that Graeme wanted to go to Dignitas, the Swiss organisation that provides an assisted suicide service to foreigners. She asked if I could talk to him.

Graeme applied to go to Dignitas, only to be rejected. I hate to admit that I did play a role in his rejection, but I felt I didn't have much choice. At Dignitas's request, I went to see Graeme at his home in Cammeray on Sydney's North Shore.

I could see why he wanted to die. He was in that terrifying period of knowing that dementia was setting in and being absolutely panic-stricken at the thought, but being too disorganised because of the dementia to do anything about it.

In my report back to Dignitas, I stated that Graeme was affected by dementia but that he also had insight into his condition. He was quite confused on some levels when I visited him, but did know he wanted to die; he said it to me over and over: 'I just want to die.' He had already made two failed attempts to kill himself: first, with a drug overdose where he took non-lethal sleeping tablets, and then by using carbon monoxide in the exhaust gas of a lawn mower. Dignitas, though, has strict rules about the mental condition of people it admits to its program, and on learning of his dementia, they rejected his application.

Caren, as Graeme's close friend, was distressed as she watched his deterioration and soon decided that enough was enough. She arranged to go to Mexico to buy Nembutal for herself and for Graeme, including a spare bottle for another Exit member who helped pay for her trip. As promised, on return Caren gave one of the Nembutal bottles to Shirley. Shirley passed it to Graeme, who poured it into his glass. His dying words were: 'Peace at last.'

While Graeme got the peaceful death he wanted, he left chaos in his wake. The doctor who'd been called to confirm the death was suspicious and refused to sign his death certificate. An autopsy was performed, and the lethal drug was found throughout Graeme's body. The question was immediately asked as to where the Nembutal had come from. Caren and Shirley had feared that this might happen and had concocted a cover story, with Caren saying her trip to Mexico had to been to visit her ailing sister, the 1950s Hollywood starlet Dana Wynter, in California. While Caren did visit Dana, the police were not convinced of her innocence. Over the next six months, the authorities tapped Caren and Shirley's phones, and in Febuary 2007, both women were arrested and charged with assisting Graeme's suicide. In a bizarre twist, neither woman was granted bail, so they spent a week in gaol at Silverwater in Sydney's west. With their joint plea of 'not guilty', a joint Supreme Court trial date was set.

At the trial preliminaries, I was informed that I would be interviewed, with the possibility I would be called as a prosecution witness. The Crown prosecutor was Mark Tedeschi QC. He is a formidable advocate, who builds cases juries tend to believe. It's not stretching things too far to say that controversy always follows him. To this day, he is the only New South Wales prosecutor who's ever faced a legal tribunal over allegations of professional misconduct (of which he would later be cleared). Infamous cases in which Tedeschi's conduct has attracted public criticism include Gordon Wood, Keli Lane and the 1990 prosecution of the 1978 Hilton bombers.[1]

On 12 May 2008, I walked into the Supreme Court of New South Wales, planning to just sit there and watch until I was needed. I was quickly asked to leave, and discovered that a witness to be called is not normally allowed to hear the proceedings before giving their evidence. So, I missed the first few days of the trial, and was worried about just what Shirley would say and whether or not she would implicate me in Caren's decision to obtain the Mexican drug. I'd had assurances from Caren that Shirley would not turn Judas, but the reports I was getting on the tactics of her QC, Peter Bodor, made me feel uncomfortable. Blaming anyone but Graeme for the mess he'd left Shirley in was understandable, but I did not want to become the sacrificial lamb. Despite a few tense moments though, Shirley was true to her word and avoided implicating others.

When I was finally called to give evidence, Tedeschi focused on a meeting I'd had with Caren and Shirley one morning on Pier 1 in The Rocks in Sydney, and I was given a rough time. He pressed hard, relentlessly trying to get me to admit that I was instrumental in Caren's decision to go to Mexico to source the drugs. As a witness, you're at a real disadvantage because you can never make much of a statement. You are expected just to answer 'yes' or 'no' to any question asked; embellishment and detail are unwelcome, especially when the prosecutor is trying to steer you in the direction he wants. Tedeschi kept pushing for an admission; I kept denying his suggestions. And he did make several blunders.

The first was almost funny, and happened when Tedeschi handed me a copy of my banned *Peaceful Pill Handbook*. I handed the book straight back to him. Accepting it, he then read from the chapter about Mexico, saying something like, 'From what you've written here, you must have known exactly what would happen when you discussed options with these women.' I replied, saying I couldn't answer that question, given that he was quoting from a banned book and I then looked at the judge, Mr Roderick Howie, for direction. His Honour asked if Mr Tedeschi had any privilege to use a banned book in the court room. Tedeschi looked blank, and looked at his junior, who also looked blank. A quick conversation about legal principles then took place and the trial seemed heading towards high farce. The jury were sent out while further legal arguments were made, with the outcome that the line of questioning based on information on Mexican Nembutal from my book was struck out.

Just as I was feeling pleased with myself for having won that round with Tedeschi, court was adjourned for the weekend. When it resumed at 10 a.m. on Monday, the ground shifted from beneath us all.

I distinctly remember sitting on the cold wooden bench outside Supreme Courtroom No. 2, in King Street, Sydney, waiting to be called to continue my evidence when people started to run backwards and forwards in an agitated way. Finally, I found the cause for all the excitement: Shirley had changed her plea to one of guilty of assisted suicide. She would tell me later she just wanted it over and was sick of watching as her experience in caring for an increasingly demented partner became fodder for the prosecution's antics. However, Tedeschi, being the hard-nosed prosecutor he was, was having none of it and refused to accept the plea change. Evidence began to emerge about Shirley's alleged lesbian relationship with a woman in Germany and her increasingly stressful time with the demented Graeme, and she seemed to have a possible new motive. Expert witnesses had begun suggesting that Graeme was too demented to make *any* decision about his future; Tedeschi joined the dots and attacked, arguing that Graeme had not suicided at all, rather that he had been murdered.

All of a sudden, Caren's world collapsed. Initially, Shirley had wanted to plead not guilty to the charge of assisting a suicide, to argue every point and tough it out. Her lawyers though had persuaded her that the wisest course was to plead guilty to this charge and try to get a lenient result. Now the women found themselves being charged with murder. Caren felt betrayed by the plea change and realised she was now part of something she could not control. From that day on, the two women sat at opposite ends of the wooden bench in the historic dock of courtroom 2.

I don't have much faith in the jury system. On the voluntary euthanasia issue particularly, I've watched as panels of my fellow citizens are made to feel that without delivering a guilty verdict, they haven't done their job. I saw it in the trial of Caren and Shirley, and I've seen it more recently, in Brisbane, when a naïve school teacher, Merin Nielsen, was found guilty of assisting in the suicide of his friend, Exit member Frank Ward.[2]

In June 2009, Merin helped Frank die, by going to Mexico and bringing Nembutal back for him. In return, Frank left his modest estate to Merin, something to which

Frank's family had agreed. Despite Frank having made his instructions, and the reasoning behind them, very clear, the jury decided that Merin was only helping Frank so that he might inherit, and found him guilty of assisting in Frank's suicide. Justice Jean Dalton said she could see no reason for leniency and sentenced Merin to three years' jail, with a non-parole period of six months. When sentencing, she said their relationship was about more than just 'philosophical chats' and that the fact that Merin was the sole beneficiary in Fred's will was 'relevant' to the sentence he would receive. As I watched the sentencing I thought, *Well who else would Frank leave his money to but his closest friend? And who else but Merin would be likely to help Frank die?* Assistance and inheritance will commonly be linked, and to suggest that they shouldn't be seems to me naïve.

In Caren and Shirley's case, the Crown suggested a similar motive, and the showman Tedeschi was just the person to do it. He played to the jury and his expert witnesses did likewise. The defence lawyers were likeable enough, but they were no match for the Crown. As Tedeschi painted Caren as evil and manipulative, her barrister, Michael Williams, QC stayed silent. The prosecutor wove a story about the type of relationship Graeme had with Shirley; about the type of friend Caren was to Graeme; and about the problematic fact that his will had all but left out his daughters from a previous marriage (Graeme had said they already got their fair share after their mother's death some years earlier). But, by the end of the evidence, Tedeschi had managed to persuade the jury to his way of thinking. Shirley was found guilty of manslaughter. Caren was found guilty of being an accessory.

During what must have been a momentary lapse of concentration on Tedeschi's part, bail was granted unopposed, with sentencing to take place in six weeks' time. While the two women were now estranged, an added complication was the attitude and behaviour of Graeme's two forty-something daughters. These women were no friends of their father's second wife. In court, they sat not in the public gallery, but with the prosecution legal team where they clearly felt most comfortable. As the likely beneficiaries of Graeme's multi-million-dollar estate, they had much riding on a guilty verdict.

Some media reports painted the whole trial as being about death, sex and money: that Shirley wanted Graeme dead so she could inherit his millions. But that begs the question: Who are you supposed to leave your worldly goods to if not the person who loves you, and who you love, the most in the world? It should come as no surprise to anyone that this special person will also be the person who helps you die.

I saw Caren fairly regularly over the intervening weeks before the sentencing date. I was often in Sydney and we'd have coffee, just as we had always done, at the Waratah Street tennis courts in Rushcutters Bay. At seventy-five, she was clever, brave and always enchanting. She was worried; she felt the stress of the trial had brought her cancer back. She was in increasing pain, and said life was an ordeal and that she craved a bit of peace. Of course what Caren was really saying, and she spelled it out clearly to me, was that she didn't want to die in jail. Who could blame her? Neither of us trusted Justice Roderick Howie to be fair; at times I thought he'd acted like a petulant child in his courtroom. Jail did seem the most likely outcome.

One day, as the sentencing date drew near, Caren said to me, 'I'm going to end my life,' and made a reference to never wanting to be handcuffed again. She knew we had a planned conference on dementia and the law in Sydney the following week to coincide with the sentencing, and asked if I would read out a statement from her—in fact, her suicide note—at that gathering. It was her choice and I knew she was serious. On Thursday, 21 September 2008, just days after her seventy-sixth birthday, Caren died peacefully and alone at her home in Lane Cove, drinking the Nembutal from the other bottle she had brought back from Mexico. Her daughter, Kate, had not known of her plans, and was heart-broken to lose her mother this way.

In retrospect, Caren was lucky to have died on her own terms, if not in her own time. Justice Howie's lengthy judg-ment vilified her, depicting her as the evil prime mover in Graeme's death. He also accused her of cowardice, for ending her life and for not facing up to her sentence. This may have worked in Shirley's favour though, and Howie seemed to soften when he moved on to her. He described her as a victim of others; meaning Caren, and, by extension, me. While his comments about Exit were unflattering, they were nothing like his denunciation of Caren. He sentenced Shirley to two years of periodic detention, with weekends in gaol in Wollongong.

Many people, particularly Graeme's daughters, saw this as an inappropriately lenient sentence. I can only imagine their disappointment when in October 2010, Shirley's appeal was upheld in the Court of Appeal and her conviction quashed. This court held that Justice Howie had erred in his instructions to the jury.

THIRTEEN

Adversaries and allies

I wonder about your friends that are not.

Rodriguez, 'I Wonder'

I've had a number of abusive letters, the odd death threat and even a bomb scare. One of the most notable occurred when I was a torchbearer in the 2000 Sydney Olympics and I needed a police escort as I did my section, jogging along McMillans Road in Darwin; a death threat had been received, the only one in the torch's long journey to Sydney. Incidents like this should be balanced with the overwhelmingly nice things that people, often total strangers, say to me in the street. But it's the nasty things that tend to stay with you. On rare occasions, I've had people getting up at meetings or in the street, yelling things like 'I'll kill you, you bastard!' In the corridors of Federal Parliament MP Bill Heffernan once shouted, 'Nitschke, you murderer!' I can't remember my reply but it must have made an impression, as some years later, when we again ran into each other in the Parliament House café, he waved me over to his table, only to tell me how he admired my tenacity.

Sometimes, public sentiment borders on the comical. Several times a year I receive envelopes with a selection of photocopied pages from the Bible, or some other religious text, threatening hell and damnation if I don't change my ways. These letters are almost inevitably anonymous and are often just addressed to 'Philip Nitschke Darwin'—but they seem to find their way to my PO box. But this is relatively easy to deal with; all sorts of public figures have to put up with total strangers having strong opinions about them. People can think what they like and I try to let the insults, when they come, wash over me.

I am fine, too, at dealing with those who clearly hate me. I've taken some of the more threatening letters I've received to the police—curious about how they will respond. They usually ask, 'Is it signed?' When I say, 'No,' the advice is, 'Well, just forget it.' I'm lucky I live in Australia. We don't, I like to think, (often) kill abortion doctors here.

Because of the nature of my work, there are always going to be incidents that upset. One recent example involved my mother, who is ninety-three and in an Adelaide nursing home. She was getting out of bed one morning, just as the GP, who had a scheduled visit, entered her room. He asked how she was and her dismissive reply was, 'I'm bloody awful, I'd rather be dead.' The next day she was told a psychiatric review was needed and the psychiatrist, his intern and a student duly arrived. Among other things, the psychiatrist asked her about her son: if she'd ever discussed euthanasia with me.

'Of course I have,' she said.

Then he asked if I'd ever advised her about specific ways of ending her life—a question she thought was inappropriate, and none of his business.

I was annoyed when I heard about this. As luck would have it, the psychiatric team did a follow-up visit on a morning that I happened to be with her. I asked about his earlier questioning of my mother, but this prompted a quick denial that the conversation had ever taken place. My mother was amazed, and said so. 'Listen. You did ask that,' she said to him, 'I may be old, but I'm not stupid.'

More troubling has been the hostility towards me from organisations as disparate as the AMA and the Australian Christian lobby, and from within the voluntary euthanasia movement itself, both here and overseas.

Many of the problems started with the announcement in 1997 of my intention to run workshops that would teach elderly Australians how to end their lives. While my opponents called for the police to act, claiming that such workshops would breach assisted suicide laws, the police held back, knowing that this area of law was grey, making a successful prosecution difficult. With the police all but silent, the complaints were then taken to the Medical Boards, urging them to remove my medical registration. Surely, they said, I was breaking my Hippocratic Oath in informing the elderly and seriously ill how they could kill themselves. Although the Oath was never administered to graduating doctors at Sydney Medical School, it was clear what my opponent's strategy was. After failing to get the police involved or criminal charges laid, the next best thing would be to have me deregistered.

By the end of 1997, I was seeing dying patients across the nation, and took out medical registration in every jurisdiction. But the complaints from religious lobby groups followed and investigations in several states were commenced. In Victoria, in 1997, the medical board sent me a formal letter asking me to show reason why I should not be disciplined, which led me to consult Robert Richter QC, who had occasionally given me legal advice. I remember Robert saying to me, 'Don't treat this too lightly, and don't hand over your medical registration without a fight, or you'll live to regret it.' The letter he drafted satisfied the board and the threat was averted, but his advice stuck in my mind. Similar incidents followed in Western Australia and South Australia, and each time I had to run around double-checking that my registration was in order, while arguing that the provision of good suicide advice is entirely consistent with good medical practice. I've been successful, and on each occasion been able to separate the running of my workshops and my medical registration. Indeed, my medical insurer, MIGA, makes a clear distinction between my medical practice and my voluntary euthanasia activities, providing no cover for the latter. Something they've done of course to protect themselves, but it is a helpful distinction for me to have on the record.

One good thing that Tony Abbott did as health minister was to amalgamate the various state registration systems, a reform that was long overdue. The stage has now changed and it is the new national body, the Australian Health Practitioners Regulatory Agency (AHPRA), that governs doctors. It is this body that is now involved in carrying out two separate long-running enquiries into my fitness to practise medicine.

While national registration may have provided some protection in Australia, this was not the case when we moved the workshop program offshore. The New Zealand Medical Registration Board, prompted by the quaintly named Society for the Protection of Community Values, wrote to me in 2001 stating that I would not be allowed to undertake a public lecture tour of that country because I was 'not licensed in New Zealand to practise medicine'! Weird. Since when is public speaking 'practising medicine'? Lawyers were involved and the tour finally went ahead, but the threat of action remains.

★ ★ ★

I dealt extensively with my views on the opposition to voluntary euthanasia from Christian churches in *Killing Me Softly*. While I'm well aware that Christianity is not one unified faith—indeed, in Exit International, there are believers of all sorts, from Catholics to Quakers, and more than a few survivors of the Holocaust—it does provide more than its fair share of my adversaries. The Australian Christian Lobby, Right to Life Australia, and the Democratic Labor Party have all rallied their troops to attack both myself and my work. The efforts of the faceless men and women of these organisations are quite insidious. They claim the moral authority of god while working the corridors of power in the State and Federal Parliaments of the nation to push their conservative moral agenda. More recently, they've even taken to lobbying statutory authorities, such as AHPRA, in their attempt to silence me and close down Exit.

Such enemies are to be expected; there is much at stake in the voluntary euthanasia debate. But it is my adversaries from within the voluntary euthanasia movement itself who often cause the greatest damage and stress. One such person was retired Queensland motel owner John Edge. His attempt to blackmail me following the much-lauded 'Peanut Project', where a group of elderly Exit members set out to synthesise their own end-of-life drugs, their own 'peaceful pill', showed me the ugly side of jealousy. It also showed how dangerous it can be to recruit others when planning an illegal event. Today, Exit has learnt from the experience. Do it yourself and you probably won't get caught; collaborate with others at your peril.

John became involved in Exit in the time leading up to the death of Nancy Crick. Nancy wanted to know whether having someone with you when you suicide could lead to them being charged with assisting. She tested the law by drinking Nembutal at her home while surrounded by twenty-one family members and friends. John had been instrumental in helping Nancy get her Nembutal and was one of those with her when she died. After watching her peaceful passing, he thought that there was no better way to go. He especially liked the idea of making his own drugs; not for today or tomorrow, but to have in the cupboard, just in case. In many late-night talks, the seed was planted. What if a group of oldies got together to make Nembutal? The organic chemistry couldn't be that hard, could it? After all, the German chemist Adolf Baeyer had first synthesised barbituric acid in his laboratory almost one hundred and fifty years earlier.

Times have changed, though. Today's plethora of back-yard drug labs and a heightened paranoia about terrorism have made it almost impossible for amateurs to acquire the equipment and chemicals needed for even the simplest synthesis. But this didn't stop the members of the Peanut Project. For specialised glassware, they simply called on the services of a retired laboratory glass blower from within the Exit community. As more people started to find out about the project, offers of help flooded in. 'You need a triple-arm flask? Sure, I'll make you one.' 'You need metallic sodium? Let me get that for you. They use that in my son's factory.' 'You need super-dry alcohol? No problem, I've got a mate who …' and so it went, not to mention, 'You need a remote farmhouse to set up the laboratory? Sure, come and use our weekender.'

After a year's careful planning, a dedicated group of twenty Exit members descended on the remote country home, in Adjungbilly, of former federal Attorney-General Kep Enderby for their big experiment. While the outcome was uncertain, it did seem possible that with the right conditions, this little group of amateur chemists might be able to pool their skills and produce their own peaceful pill.

Accounts tell of an almost party-like atmosphere on the night, and the group did succeed in producing barbituric acid (subsequent lab tests proved this), but they fell short of producing the desired sodium pentobarbital or Nembutal, the prized euthanasia drug. To get technical for a moment, the critical molecular side-chain had refused to stick and the crystals had not formed, although everyone participating believed they had. What they didn't know though, was that John had taken it upon himself, under the cover of darkness, to spike the mixture after discovering that the sediment was lacking. I remember when he first told me, and of my immediate concern. While the powder they'd all taken home might just be lethal if swallowed, a death as a result may be far from peaceful.

From this point, John's and my relationship rapidly deteriorated. He claimed that I had declared the project an Exit success (which I had thought it was), and accused me of duplicity. He wanted to tell the story, but in his way. After all, he said, you weren't there. Eventually, I suggested we write up the story for Exit's newsletter, *Deliverance*, and rang John from Sydney to seek his support. He said, 'You'll do that over my dead body. If you write anything, I'm going to the police, and you're dead.' It wasn't an idle threat. I feared he had documents and records that could show my involvement in the planning part of the conspiracy to synthesise illegal drugs. I hung up and felt sick; we never spoke again.

By this stage the Peanut Project had lost its appeal. It was simply too risky for any of the participants to keep the drugs they had made, and after Edge's threat, too risky to carry out the necessary further chemical modification. As a result, all samples were collected and destroyed—a huge disappointment for everyone involved. It wasn't part of the deal for those present to have their plans sabotaged and to find themselves facing considerable legal risk, because of one man's ego. The last I heard of John was that he'd taken his life one night in a Gold Coast cemetery in 2010, using helium and a plastic bag, a method he had once scorned.

While this is just one case of what can go wrong when working alongside a colleague in the voluntary euthanasia movement, there are many other examples of people who I barely even know who have been the saboteurs. People who, like me, believe in having end of life choice, but who often have a radically different take on how to get it.

The right-to-die movement is philosophically divided into two camps, with a few undecideds in between. At the crux of the split is a disagreement over whether the option of a peaceful death should be reserved for those who are terminally (or at least seriously) ill, or whether we are really talking about a fundamental human right, available to all who understand death (i.e. not children or those mentally impaired), whether sick or not. The role of the medical profession depends on which side of the divide you stand. Those who see voluntary euthanasia as an option restricted to the sick, invariably place the medical profession at centre stage. It is doctors who will decide if the person is sick enough to qualify; it is doctors who will prescribe the lethal drugs or administer the fatal injection. Those who would argue that a peaceful death is a fundamental matter of personal choice often see little point in involving a profession whose whole recorded history has focused on saving and prolonging life.

I have found my own position changing. I entered the debate believing that the only way forward was for the passage of legislation such at the Northern Territory's ROTI Act, which would allow only the terminally ill access to lawful help to die. And, as a doctor, I would be one of those chosen to judge the applicants, and ultimately to provide the necessary assistance. But even at that early stage, my beliefs were being challenged. It was Bob Dent who first made the point. 'Why do I have to see a psychiatrist?' he complained. 'If I had the drugs, I could just take them when the time was right, no doctors or psychiatrists needed.' He was of course right, and I felt guilty as I dragged him and three other terminally ill patients around Darwin seeing the doctors needed to sign their papers in order to use the Territory law. Why couldn't he, I reasoned, have his own Nembutal locked in his cupboard to take if and when he wanted. After all, as a doctor I had access to the drug, and what gave me that right? Indeed shouldn't all adults have access to that drug?

This philosophical split is not new, and it is enduring. For as long as I can remember, I have been criticised each time I have dared to suggest that you don't need a person in a white coat alongside your bed when you die. That is, you don't need a doctor to die—you can actually do it yourself.

In Australia, the fissure first emerged in Melbourne as early as 1998, when the Voluntary Euthanasia Society of Victoria, then led by Dr Rodney Syme, 'distanced' itself from what were reported as my 'more direct' methods—the so-called 'technical' solution—and the development of the 'suicide' or 'peaceful' pill.[1] By early 2002 the split was widening, with the Melbourne society deciding that a person's right to access information (and thereby the means of a peaceful death outside of the medical profession) was 'incompatible' with their charter. The controversial death in 2002 of healthy retired French academic Lisette Nigot drew more attention to the issue. Nigot took her own life purely because she was turning eighty and had long said 'eighty was the time to go'. Rational suicide, with no underlying medical reason. The Nigot controversy would be repeated at the end of 2012, with healthy eighty-nine-year-old Exit member Susan Potts. Susan was the elder sister of Sara Henderson, of Bullo Station, who had written the best-selling *From Strength to Strength* about her own struggle with breast cancer. Like Lisette, Susan also decided that rational suicide was for her, and elected not to involve the medical profession in her death.

As the split widened, Rodney Syme laid his cards on the table, stating that his main concern was to ensure the medical profession remained central to the death of a person. 'Euthanasia', he said, was a 'medical problem' that needed the 'right kind of doctors' to assist those who wanted to die. A peaceful pill, Syme wrote in his book, was a 'pathway to disaster'.[2] Hearing him on the radio, I remember thinking to myself, *At last, you've made your position clear.*[3]

However, there is more to Rodney's objection to my non-medical, do-it-yourself approach than meets the eye. For almost two decades, he has been beseeching the law to take a good hard look at his involvement with dying patients, actively seeking to be investigated and charged. He even appeared in fake handcuffs on the front cover of the *Bulletin* magazine, with the sensational headline 'Arrest Me', after admitting to giving lethal drugs to several terminally ill patients. While some may see this as a brave doctor challenging the law while helping the sick, to me it shows an insufferable paternalism that strips the patient of their last vestige of control. Syme, or any doctor, who gives Nembutal to a dying patient may argue that this is fine because, under the medical model, it is the doctor who knows best and who should make the decision. However, this means it is the doctor, rather than the patient— the dying person—who determines who should die peacefully and who should not. In this scenario, no rational adult person can ever be entrusted with the decision about ending their own life. This focus on the central role of doctors has restricted the euthanasia debate and turned it into an argument about disease, mental capacity, safeguards and access.

Who is sick enough to qualify? Who should be rejected? From this viewpoint an important point is lost: death is not a legal nor a medical procedure; it is a natural, social and cultural event that we will all experience. And it is one that we should not abandon control of. Who says that the legislators and the medical establishment should be the gatekeepers? Not me.

I believe that every rational adult should have access to a reliable, peaceful and lethal pill that one keeps at home. Use of this pill would only be considered when one finds that the quality of life is such that death *is* the preferred option. This is how it should be, how it could be. Surely the most effective way of ensuring that control of the process remains with the person who wishes to die. It is a radical proposal that decouples death and disease and one that acknowledges that there can be powerful and compelling non-medical reasons to seek death, reasons that have nothing at all to do with disease. Surely this could be seen as a measure of maturity in society, the exact antithesis of the controls of a nanny state. I suspect, however, that the devolution of responsibility to rational elderly adults for the timing and manner of their deaths is not a goal many doctors or politicians will seek.

I have also found myself in ideologically treacherous waters on the other side of the world. In May 2009 Exit held its first workshop in Glasgow. The meeting, at the Glasgow Unitarian Church, was well promoted by the media and well attended on the day. While there was the usual scaremongering and moral panic from the traditional churches, we also had an extra adversary, in the form of Dr Libby Wilson, convenor of the Scottish pro-euthanasia group FATE (Friends at the End). In both television and print, Libby castigated me for suggesting that every rational adult over the age of fifty should be entrusted with their own end-of-life decisions. She said, 'Most people feel quite revolted by [his approach].'[4] She told the Glasgow *Herald*: 'He's done a terrible lot of harm in Australia … [T]he reaction to him [there] has been absolutely draconian … He makes it slightly difficult for those of us who want to stick to our ethical standards.'[5] All the while, Dr Wilson was billing herself as 'dedicated to promoting knowledge about end-of-life choices'.

A month after my Glasgow workshop, Wilson purchased a subscription to *The Peaceful Pill eHandbook* and, later, she bought multiple print copies as well. What I fail to understand is why it is all right for her to have this information, but not others? It is more than just hypocrisy; it is using medical privilege to exclude the majority of the population. These arguments were played out compellingly in Janine Hosking's documentary, *Mademoiselle and the Doctor*. I met retired French academic Lisette (Mademoiselle) Nigot in Perth in 1998. She explained that although she was not ill, she did not want to live past the age of eighty. Four years later, and shortly before her eightieth birthday, she ended her life with barbiturates she had acquired. In those four years I got to know her well. She constantly challenged my right to withhold information. Any suggestion that I knew what was best for her, because of my medical training, was dismissed with contempt; at one point she threatened to sack me as her doctor if I didn't impart the information that I had and she wanted. I could see no legitimate reason to argue; it was her decision to make, not mine.

With friends like Drs Syme and Wilson, you've got to ask, who needs enemies? Another UK adversary is retired GP Michael Irwin. A former chairman of the UK Voluntary Euthanasia Society (now called Dignity in Dying), Irwin had been keen to find out all he could about Nembutal, contacting me in 2008 to provide him with details on sources of the drug in Mexico and Southeast Asia. It came then as something of a shock to learn a year later, during our 2009 UK tour, that he was now accusing me in *The Telegraph* of being 'totally irresponsible' by telling the rational elderly adults at my workshops how they might get Nembutal from Mexico. But why should he be the one who decides who should, or should not, access such information? More recently, Irwin has established a new group that continues to place the medical profession firmly at the centre of the decision-making process. Under his model, a rational elderly person wanting a 'doctor-assisted suicide' would need to be interviewed by two doctors (one a consultant geriatrician), appoint an official legal witness, and then be subject to a two-month cooling-off period. The final act of suicide would need to be committed in the presence of a doctor, rather than an 'unqualified relative or friend as (according to Dr Irwin) there is a great danger that mistakes will occur'. Finally, the death would require detailed reporting to a central government office.

Bureaucracy such as this sits badly with many elderly folk, who think it's no one else's business when and how they die. With first-hand experience of a voluntary euthanasia law, I saw the way legislation made my terminally ill patients jump

Clockwise from top My mother Gwen, 1939 (personal collection); citizen's arrest, 1965 (*The Advertiser*); graduation with honours in physics, University of Adelaide, 1967 (personal collection); school portrait, Peterborough Primary (personal collection)

From left My sister Gailene, her husband Bill, my mother and father Gwen and Harold, Jenny and my brother Dennis, Adelaide, 1969 (personal collection)

With Jenny and the new Bolwell, Flinders University, 1971 (personal collection)

Home, Wattie Creek, Northern Territory, 1973 (personal collection)

Above Tram conducting didn't teach me what I needed to know, 1975

Right Parks and Wildlife ranger, Alice Springs, 1979 (personal collection)

'DEATH RAY' FEARS

So nuclear scientist 'drops out'

7—SUNDAY MAIL, May 27, 1973

BRITAIN WORKING ON 'DEATH RAY'

A laser ray is being developed as a "death ray" as the most powerful weapon in the armoury, according to Chapman Pincher, science editor of the Daily Express.

The ray could be used to destroy planes, missiles, and tanks, he said, quoting a Defence Ministry spokesman. The system uses powerful laser beams which can punch holes through metal at long range.

Physicist Dr. Philip Nitschke stopped his world of lasers and nuclear energy three months ago and got off.

And that is how two young South Australians found paradise for $10 a week.

Philip is 25 and his wife, Jenny, 24.

For four months they have lived at remote Cape du Couedic on Kangaroo Island, tucked away in the magnificent scrubland of Flinders Chase, the 135,680-acre wildlife reserve.

Their closest acquaintances are wallabies, a possum or two, a score or more seals, a few goannas, some bats ... and an aloof osprey.

With this company, the Nitschkes have been taking a long, hard look at the world, people, and themselves.

Their idyll arose out of—fears that man may ill-use one of science's most remarkable tools, the laser.

It has long been called the death ray, capable of vaporising man or metal.

At Flinders University Philip's work involved the laser and he believed its development was at the stage where military interest was aroused.

He felt the laser could develop into the death ray, hitherto the province of science fiction writers.

Then a breakthrough in power generation for the laser triggered his fears.

He did not like what he saw.

"I could not see what possible good my scientific contribution was going to do for society," he explains.

So he decided to get off the wheel.

He took the job as caretaker of Flinders University's oceanographic research station at Cape de Couedic ... $5 a week and house provided.

For reading: weather instruments he gets another $5.

Story P. 34

Building threat to SA

The Sydney building dispute could spread to SA, Building and Construction Workers' Federation secretary Mr. L. J. Robinson warned last night.

Federal Housing Minister, Mr. Johnson, said yesterday the dispute had reached crisis point.

He said he hoped a Federal Government suggestion for an independent enquiry into union claims for permanent employment would be accepted by both parties—the Master Builders' Association and the Builders' Laborers' Federation.

Mr. Robinson said a Government inquiry would be welcome—as would permanency in the industry in all States.

"Building workers generally want permanency in some form in the industry," he said.

"If the dispute in NSW continues, and the Master Builders will not recognise what the workers want, the dispute could well spread."

The national executive of the Builders' Laborers' Federation have been asked to discuss the matter with the Housing Minister and several other Ministers in Canberra on Tuesday.

Federation executives have been called to a compulsory conference before the conciliation and arbitration commission in Canberra on Tuesday.

Already 6,000 tradesmen and 4,000 laborers have been dismissed or stood down from building sites in Sydney.

Mr. Johnson said the national interest could be affected as well as those directly involved. A compromise had to be reached.

On the permanent employment inquiry, Mr. Johnson said:

"If such a course would satisfy the unions and meets with the proper response from the Master Builders', it seems that we will not only be able to avert a national crisis, but also pave the way to solving a sociological issue."

Free

All you want to know about Alutile or Tylox roofing tiles.

Four take to liferafts after yacht founders

Above 'Nuclear scientist drops out', 1975 (courtesy Newspix)

Inset Just before she went belly up: *Squizz*, 1990 (courtesy Newspix)

Doctor Fallout

An insider who exposed Darwin Hospital's lack of
readiness for a nuclear accident still feels the heat

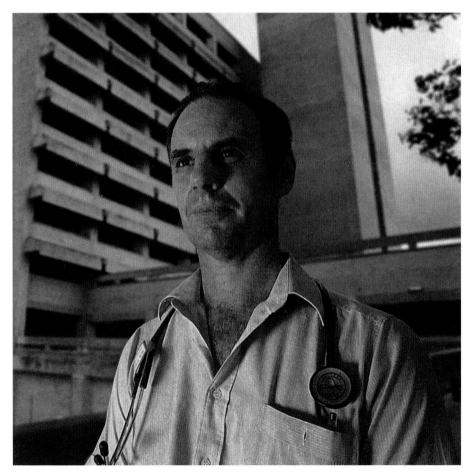

'Free Speech?' banner drapes over Royal Darwin Hospital in protest over nuclear ships
dismissal, as reported in *Time* magazine, 2003 (courtesy *Time*/David Hancock)

Burning the ROTI Act,
Parliament House steps,
Canberra, 1997 (courtesy
Julian Kingma/John
Fairfax Publications)

Philip sitting in front
of the three-storey high
billboard of 'My Beautiful
Chair' (MONA) as
displayed on the Republic
Building in Melbourne's
CBD (personal collection)

Above Moral outrage in Ireland, 2011 (personal collection)

Invitation to the Festival of Dangerous Ideas, 2011 (courtesy Ideas at the House (Sydney Opera House))

On the campaign trail for the Sex Party in the NT election, 2012 (personal collection)

Fiona and me and the Russian Cossack, at William Creek on the Oodnadatta track, 2007 (personal collection)

Right For \$20—a taco, a tequila margarita and a bottle of Nembutal: Tijuana, Mexico, 2005 (personal collection)

Below With Fiona Stewart, 'the cream in my coffee', and Henny Penny, 2012 (Dave Hancock)

through hoops. Law reform strategies that advocate safeguards to the 'nth' degree may find appeal with politicians trying to appease their opponents, but they are inherently flawed.

Another prominent UK activist to attack Exit workshops is Debbie Purdy. Debbie, aged fifty, suffers from multiple sclerosis and is best known as the English woman who has booked herself into Dignitas. She went to the English High Court in 2008 to ensure that should her husband accompany her to Zurich for her assisted suicide, he would not be prosecuted on his return to the UK. She won this important case, a result that was instrumental in the decision in 2009 for the Director of Public Prosecution, Kier Starmer, to issue guidelines on the likelihood of prosecution in future assisted suicide cases.

Debbie has spoken at length about the importance of control. In a 2012 interview in *The Financial Times*, she said, 'Dignity is about being in control. The thing is, you've got to understand the stress. You feel unable to get up in the morning if you have no autonomy.'[6] Given that Exit workshops are all about restoring an individual's autonomy by ensuring that people have control, her repeated attacks on Exit and myself seem misplaced. To Debbie, Exit's workshops are 'dangerous'.[7] Indeed, she has said: 'If someone decides their life is unbearable and they want to die, they ought to be able to find out how to do it, but they also must be told why it might not be right for them'. She went on, 'It is important that proper safeguarded discussions are had with medical professionals and people who can offer alternatives—and that isn't something that is going to happen at these (Exit) lectures.'[8]

I have found myself speaking in opposition to Debbie in debates and interviews in the UK and as far away as Hong Kong, despite the fact that we seem to share many of the same ideas. To date, she has declined repeated invitations to come along to a workshop, and hear the arguments and my approach for herself.

In the US, although the same divisions within the assisted suicide movement exist, there has been a much greater level of acceptance of Exit DIY strategies. Indeed it was on one of my earlier visits to North America in 1998 when I took part in a landmark meeting in Victoria on Vancouver Island with two other activists: John Hofsess and Rob Neals from Oregon. At that meeting a decision was made to set up Nu-Tech, a group dedicated to researching and developing technologies that would provide individuals with means to end their lives unassisted—self-deliverance. We each brought our specific fields of interest to that meeting; John, with his enthusiasm for a device he called the 'De-breather', which would deliver a peaceful death from hypoxia, and Rob, with his interest in the use of inert gases such as helium to achieve the same goal. My interest was (and still is) in the development of a 'peaceful pill', something that can be taken easily and lead to an inevitable and peaceful death. Indeed I first spoke on this concept, coining the phrase 'peaceful pill', when I addressed the 1998 World Federation of Right to Die Societies conference in Zurich.

Nu Tech grew quickly, especially when it was joined, and for some time largely funded, by Derek Humphry, the long-term activist who had published the important self-help book *Final Exit*. My subsequent visits to the US and Canada were often made to coincide with Nu-Tech gatherings, and in the early stages of the group, valuable information was shared. In recent years, the group has faltered, coat-tailing on the biannual World Federation of Right to Die conferences, and becoming little more than a gathering where anecdotes are shared, rather than research presented.

With its large ageing population and strong right-to-die movement, North America remains important to Exit. This became very clear in September 2006 when the *Peaceful Pill Handbook* was launched at the Toronto World Federation conference. With a write-up in *The New York Times*, the handbook made Amazon's top 100 bestselling list. This was followed two years later with the online handbook, and strong North American sales have continued ever since. This reflects, I believe, the considerable interest Americans have in the published sections about how to get Nembutal along the US–Mexican border. This was new information, unavailable in books like *Final Exit*, and it served a need. As an online book, we upgrade the section on Mexico every time new information comes in. At every revision, there is a surge in popularity.

Exit workshops were launched in America to satisfy the demand for information ignited by the *Peaceful Pill Handbook*. In 2009 the first workshop series ran with great success in Los Angeles, Washington State and San Francisco. But a follow-up trip to launch in Florida and New York never happened. I'm not sure what I did wrong, or whether it could have been averted, but the decision in 2010 to refuse my application for a US visa forced the cancellation of the proposed tour and caused immense difficulty.

By 2012 things were back on track, and with a US tourist visa I was able to attend San Diego Beer Week, although the Sydney consulate made me undertake a verbal assurance that no meetings would be held. The beer was great, and I held to my promise not to hold any meetings. But being that close to the Mexican border meant it was easy to walk over to Tijuana and carry out some Nembutal fieldwork, which was then published in the December 2012 handbook update. While America remains Exit's largest audience, the question on how best to run a workshop tour there remains unanswered.

★ ★ ★

As is frequently the case in the non-profit sector, when there is ideology and the charity dollar is at stake, divisions and hostilities are often not far away. In Australia, this was particularly evident at the time of the death of property developer and former Lord Mayor of Brisbane Clem Jones, in

2007. After Clem died, his will stated he was leaving a cool five million to the voluntary euthanasia movement. Jones' will stated:

> I instruct my Executors to provide Five Million Dollars ($5 000 000) to use in whatever way they see fit to help those who are fighting to enable those who have suffered as I have described (and most of us have experienced), who choose to end their lives, to do so and to make it lawful and to provide within our laws, the ways and means for this to happen within the law.

Back in 2003, I had tried hard to amalgamate Australia's seven state-based voluntary euthanasia societies. While it made good political sense to have one united voice, a new national group would have meant seven little kings and queens giving up their respective feifdoms, this was never going to happen, and the group was never formed. Instead, Exit International established its own national chapter, or branch, network and has grown to be the only national voluntary euthanasia member organisation in Australia.

No sooner had Clem's will been made public than I started receiving media calls asking how it felt to be the recipient of such largesse. I was careful to say that, while it was great for the movement, I had no knowledge of how Exit would fare until I talked to lawyers. Herein lay the next shock. On talking to a few equity silks who pored over the structure of the Jones will, it was clear that neither Exit, nor any other group, was a beneficiary. The handful of trustees had sole discretion as to who would get the money and for what.

At this point, Marshall Perron appeared back on the scene; even though he was long retired to the Sunshine Coast hinterland, he emailed, asking if I would allow him to represent Exit to the Clem Jones trustees. I was flabbergasted. Perron had all but dropped out of the voluntary euthanasia movement since his retirement from politics in 1996. This had always surprised me, given the passion with which he had pushed his world-changing legislation through the Northern Territory parliament. But, I reasoned, he felt he had done enough. Even when he failed to turn up in Canberra to watch the debate that would finally bury his ROTI Act, I wasn't that surprised. But here he was now, fifteen years later, offering to act as an agent on our behalf, to ensure that Exit got a slice of the Clem Jones pie. I declined the offer, saying we would present our own case, but I felt uneasy, and knew something was afoot. It soon became clear. Like some giant magnet, the Clem Jones money pulled together the state voluntary euthanasia societies, something I had never been able to do. Sensing a cash cow, they all fell into line, eliciting the services of Marshall Perron and agreeing to employ a little-known lobbyist, Neal Francis, on a $100 000-plus annual salary to form a so-called new 'national peak body'.

Three years later, this group 'YourLastRight', had little to show for itself, and its lack of progress had not gone unnoticed. In 2012, the West Australian Voluntary Euthanasia Society resigned from the group in disgust, amid allegations of financial impropriety.[9] Dying with Dignity NSW also voiced its concern, and when long-term president of the Queensland society John Todd was forced to resign, the questions really started to flow. In the August 2012 editorial in our newsletter *Deliverance*, I joined those daring to ask what had become of Clem Jones' 'missing millions',[10] and immediately received a letter from the group's CEO and chairman, Neal Francis, threatening legal action for defamation. While I mulled over whether or not I had anything to apologise for, the disintegration of YourLastRight began.

In September 2012, the online news service Crikey.com published an account of the events leading to the abortive defamation action against myself and Exit.[11] With this publicity the executors of the estate became decidedly nervous and froze further funding to YourLastRight. Francis would resign from his position as president of Dying with Dignity Victoria ten days after the defamation threat arrived in my inbox. While Francis cited 'personal reasons' for the resignation, Rodney Syme would later state in an email to me that the real reason was that the defamation action 'did not have the endorsement of his Committee', all of whom were listed as co-litigants on notice of defamation. On 11 December 2012, Francis resigned from his remaining positions as chairman and CEO of YourLastRight and finally the World Federation of Right to Die Societies. While the group (now minus the support of several key players) may be able to survive in some form, the question of how the Clem Jones millions are to be spent remains unanswered, and a matter of concern to all Australian supporters of voluntary euthanasia.

The politics around the Clem Jones legacy brought out the worst in the movement. The public spectacle of internal squabbling among those who are essentially on the same side, with groups denouncing one another on the basis of mistruths and smear was in no one's interest. The South Australian Voluntary Euthanasia Society took the prize, printing on all the newsletter bannerheads and on their website that they are 'not affiliated with Exit International/Dr Philip Nitschke and opposes [sic] the public availability of a "peaceful pill"'. The mischievous imputation, of course, is that I'd make a peaceful pill available to all who wanted it, including depressed teens. While I expect such mud-slinging from the religious fundamentalists and Right to Life supporters, pro-choice advocates should know, and act, better.

The allegation about suicide pills for depressed teens stems from a 2001 interview I did with Kathryn Jean Lopez, for the conservative but influential US magazine *National Review*.

Lopez asked me:

Do you see any restrictions that should be placed on euthanasia generally? If I am depressed, do I qualify? If an elderly woman's husband dies and she says she no longer has anything to live for, would you help her kill herself? What about a troubled teen? Who qualifies? Who decides if a life is worth living?

I responded:

This difficult question I will answer in two parts. My personal position is that if we believe that there is a right to life, then we must accept that people have a right to dispose of that life whenever they want. (In the same way as the right to freedom of religion has implicit the right to be an atheist, and the right to freedom of speech involves the right to remain silent.) I do not believe that telling people they have a right to life while denying them the means, manner, or information necessary for them to give this life away has any ethical consistency. So all people qualify, not just those with the training, knowledge or resources to find out how to 'give away' their life. And someone needs to provide this knowledge, training, or recourse necessary to anyone who wants it, including the depressed, the elderly bereaved, [and] the troubled teen. If we are to remain consistent and we believe that the individual has the right to dispose of their life, we should not erect artificial barriers in the way of sub-groups who don't meet our criteria.

This would mean that the so-called 'peaceful pill' should be available in the supermarket so that those old enough to understand death could obtain death peacefully at the time of their choosing. It's hard to imagine

how such a development would affect society, but I
believe the impact would not be as great as people fear
...

The final question that needs to be answered
though is 'Whom do I want to help?' While acknowl-
edging that all have the 'right' to receive assistance without fear of legal consequence, I do not personally want
to involve myself in helping those who can manage the
act themselves. The purpose of the deliverance machine
... was to allow the individual to initiate the process and
to take the responsibility for their actions. My guidelines
for those whom I am prepared to assist are of course
arbitrary. In this country, without protective legislation,
I could do what I liked, or rather, what I could get away
with. However, *I choose to restrict myself* to that group
identified in the overturned legislation. I involve myself
with terminally ill adults who are articulate, lucid, and
not suffering from clinically treatable depression.[12]

From this interview, in which I was philosophising about
end-of-life choices, a furore has arisen about what I really
meant by my now infamous 'supermarket shelf' statement.
This interview gave the Christian Right a free kick, but I was
much more surprised when those who are supposedly on my
side used the same technique to attack me. In mid 2012, the
Clem Jones bequest to the voluntary euthanasia movement
legally 'failed', and the financial playing field is once again
level. It is hard work raising the monies required to fund an
advocacy organisation on a so-called moral issue like voluntary euthanasia. If, in the future, there is another windfall of
this magnitude, it would help immensely if decisions about
where money then flows could be decided by the quality of
the suggested ideas for change, along with their ability to be
strategically implemented. However, I'm not naïve enough
to think this will likely be the case.

Ultimately, criticism of me from within the voluntary euthanasia movement is a distraction (I'm not perfect and my public actions and statements are not always understood, or properly reported in the media). Responding to accusations could become a full time job if I let it. But this should not distract me from what is the main game: fighting the real opponents, those who would deny us choice over how we live and die.

FOURTEEN

My life with the media

He must have a long spoon that must eat with the devil.

William Shakespeare, *The Comedy of Errors*

In some ways, I've been lucky having been exposed to the media from a relatively young age. If my citizen's arrest at the age of sixteen years taught me anything, it was that what is reported is not necessarily an accurate description of the facts: an insight that has stood me in good stead ever since. While I might have had some powerful winning media moments on the topic of voluntary euthanasia, I've also had some spectacular failures and even stuff-ups. In addition, social media has provided new and undreamt of ways to allow the failures in particular to live on.

To those on the outside, it seems that harnessing the media on behalf of a social issue such as voluntary euthanasia takes nothing more than a phone call to a friendly journalist. Exit members are constantly surprised when I tell them I have little or no control over what the newspapers write about me or the debate more broadly. I find myself forever explaining that 'Yes, it was unfortunate that "Cheryl" from *The Australian* missed this or that vital point'. Or that she failed to mention Exit by name. Or that this or that politician has now gone back on their word. Although often annoying, as the writer WH Auden once remarked, what the mass media offers is 'entertainment which is intended to be consumed like food, forgotten, and replaced by a new dish'.

Over the past fifteen years, my experience of, and life in, the media has crossed cultural and language divides. From Russian state television, or cable television in mainland China, to local school children interviewing me for high school assignments. Then there has been US primetime news on CNN with the ruthless Connie Chung and the outright sensationalism in the UK's now-defunct *News of the World*. In all I have been propped up, shot down, admired and loathed. Sometimes the voluntary euthanasia issue wins out, and my point has shone through; the focus is on the message, not the messenger. At other times though, I have been depicted as a murderous, bloodthirsty doctor who is getting filthy rich on killing innocent elderly members of the community. 'Aren't you making a lot of money out of death?' is a question BBC journalists, in particular, seem concerned with.

The angles the media have covered have ranged widely, as have the large number of Exit members who have bravely spoken out prior to ending their lives: Chris Rossiter, Don and Iris Flounders, Angie Belecciu, Dr John Elliott, Steve Guest, Lisette Nigot, Sandy Williamson, Norma Hall, Jay Franklin, Angelique Flowers, Nancy Crick, Caren Jenning, Susan Potts and many, many others. Issues covered include the four deaths of my patients under the ROTI Act, Exit workshop and meeting venue closures, the banning of *The Peaceful Pill Handbook* and television advertisements, and DIY technologies such as my Nitrogen system (marketed as Max Dog Brewing cylinders—Max being a rather gormless red heeler dog that a good friend of mine owns). And then there has been the police raids on Exit's Australian offices, trips to Tijuana with terminally ill Exit members, internet hacking workshops, Nembutal test kits, teenage deaths from Nembutal, court trials, parliamentary apologies, and street demonstrations and protests. In only a small minority of these events have I been able to set the agenda and watch the media blindly follow. Invariably one finds oneself buffeted by the media wind, with little certainty of the eventual outcome. Nowhere was this more obvious than in 2004, with the death of Gold Coast grandmother Nancy Crick from a Nembutal overdose.

The fall-out from Nancy's death continues to this day; media reports ensure that she is remembered as the granny who was tricked into thinking she was terminally ill, and then helped to die. My role in the 'cover-up' was in telling the media she had bowel cancer when I should have stressed that she was in fact suffering from the effects of 'successful' cancer surgery, thus explaining why the quickie autopsy by the Queensland Coroner's office showed she had died 'cancer free'. Who could blame the person in the street for being more than a little confused?

In *Killing Me Softly*, I wrote about the circumstances of Nancy's death in some detail. I wrote, too, about the political opportunism of any number of commentators, and in particular, the then Queensland Premier Peter Beattie.

My efforts to pitch Nancy's story to a variety of media worked well. The press releases were picked up and run with, and the strategically placed phone calls to a chosen few journalists had their desired effect. It was a story with a very human face. Here was your sixty-something battler, a retired barmaid from the working-class suburb of Brunswick in inner Melbourne. Nancy had seen a lot of life, and had more than her share of bad luck, with her husband, Jimmy, dying just as they both should have been enjoying their retirement in the sun.

The coverage of Nancy's story about wanting to die grew organically and she was fast on her way to becoming a household name, presenting a hard-to-argue-with case as she spoke to local and national newspapers, and appeared on Channel 9's *A Current Affair*. We held a public meeting on the

Gold Coast, and Nancy even launched an internet diary, with which she was in touch with an ever-increasing number of friends and strangers (including a hospice patient in Venice, a farmer in the US and even a fisherman from the Falkland Islands) about her quality of life, her plans for the future and whether or not she would take that final step.

While I was happy enough for the media to follow Nancy's every move while she was alive, common sense told me that media presence on the day of her intended death was always going to be tacky. Who wants to die on film? Who wants their death to be a tabloid sensation, and fodder for breakfast- and dinner-table chat throughout the nation (and the world)? Once Nancy had decided on the time and day, the management of the media became of particular concern. To gain some control I leaked that there was a range of possible dates. Subterfuge became the name of the game as I tried to shake the media's now-obsessive focus on Nancy's pending death. At this point, a number of us from Exit even bought prepaid mobile phones, so our planning conversations would be kept private from both the media and the police.

In one way, I was successful, Nancy died at home in private, surrounded by those twenty-one people she cared about. No one ever discovered just where, or when, she acquired her Nembutal, although this was not the point. Nancy wanted her death to mean something. She wanted to challenge the law. She wanted to know if those who were with her when she died would be charged with assisting her suicide, simply because they were present when she took that final step. This was a question I also wanted the Queensland authorities to address. Many people want those they love around them when they die, but no one wants their family subject to legal risk by so doing. Clarification of what does or does not constitute 'assisting' is important. Unfortunately, the unexpected aftermath of Nancy's death has left this question unanswered.

After months of micro-managing the media around
Nancy, all hell broke loose. My image, as the caring human
rights activist, was reinvented as a duplicitous manipulator
who would stop at nothing for his own self-aggrandisement.
In *Killing Me Softly*, I wrote:

> Nancy's death was bound to be a high-profile, political
> affair. Despite this fact, few could have foreseen the way
> in which the preliminary results of her autopsy would
> be leaked to the public in an attempt to damage my
> reputation. I learnt of the leak when I received a phone
> call from a senior journalist with *The Courier-Mail*
> newspaper just forty-eight hours after Nancy's death.
> His comments shocked me. 'Very reliable sources', he
> said, had leaked to him the news that a government
> pathologist at Brisbane's John Tonge Forensic Centre
> had reported he could find no trace of cancer in Mrs
> Crick's body. 'This,' he said, 'changed everything.'

What wasn't discussed was the fine distinction between
suffering from 'having cancer' and suffering caused from the
major surgery needed to remove the cancer. Did the surgery
get all the cancer? This question was never addressed, and nor
was the issue of the abdominal adhesions, the painful scarring
that was left after her 'successful cancer surgery'.

But, to me, what was most shocking was that an autopsy
had been arranged so quickly, and that the 'results' of what
could only have been the most superficial of examinations
were at *The Courier-Mail* before Nancy's body had cooled.
Autopsies take time to arrange and time to execute, and it
takes weeks to carry out the microscopic, histological and
biochemical examinations necessary to establish accurately a
cause of death. And, besides, test results are confidential until
the coroner makes his or her decision about the need, or

otherwise, for an inquest. So, how did it happen that just three days after Nancy's death the major Australian newspapers began running the headline 'Crick Died Cancer Free'?[1] There was a stench about this; influence had clearly been exercised at the highest level.

To this day, I think it is of little importance whether Nancy still had her cancer when she died; suffering is suffering. Nancy also saw the question as being of little significance, and I think certain media representatives found it convenient to ignore the fact that even Nancy was ambivalent about her actual status regarding the cancer. Two months before her death, in an interview with journalist Leisa Scott in *The Weekend Australian*, Nancy had said:

> I don't know what I've got and they don't know what I've got, but whatever it is, it's bloody well there. And they can't find it with their operations and in the end it comes down to quality of life and I've got none of that now. Those who keep telling me what to do aren't going through what I'm going through. It's not up to the politicians, or the church or the doctors, it's up to the people, and it's up to the patients. Why don't they ask the people?[2]

But for a government embarrassed on an almost daily basis by this suffering woman and her public diary and wanting to hide its own inadequacy, and a society preferring not to have to deal with the awful reality that life after 'successful' cancer surgery can be worse than the cancer itself, truth was of little importance. Many media reports condemned me. The AMA's deputy president, Trevor Mudge, sermonised that 'you have to look at the quality of the advice she's been offered', while other nameless 'leading surgeons' were said to have 'expressed concern' about my diagnosis.[3] I was being portrayed as a person who had used Nancy and her family to serve my own ambitions, and, even worse, to have lied to the Australian public.

Of course, none of these accusations were true, as the article in *The Weekend Australian* had made clear. *No one* had known exactly what the situation was with Nancy's health. All we knew was that she had a problem and that she— not I—felt her life was not worth living as a result. Yet, the Queensland Premier of the day, Peter Beattie couldn't resist the opportunity to sink the boot in, stating, 'I just say to the learned doctor, you've got a lot of explaining to do'. He then went in for some more point scoring, suggesting that 'legalised euthanasia could be misused by some people to attempt to murder their relatives'.[4]

The stress of the attacks from the media, and from Beattie and the AMA, was huge, but at this most difficult time, Marshall Perron came to my aid. As someone with many years experience in the head-kicking and back-stabbing that is Australian politics, he rang me and simply said, 'Don't be too discouraged. You only cop this sort of flak when you're over the target.'

I spent quite a bit of time in the days that followed, feeling sorry for myself and licking my wounds. In retrospect, it's clear that I should have publicly stressed to a much greater degree that I didn't know, and indeed, it didn't matter to Nancy, whether it was the cancer or the cancer treatment that had destroyed her quality of life. The point was, with no quality of life and no relief in sight, death, in her view, had become the best option. I was again made to realise that when you tangle with powerful forces, and with people used to playing the dirty games of politics and power, you can really get hurt. What was also made crystal clear to me was that governments will do everything they can to destroy the integrity and credibility of those who draw attention to the administration's inadequacy. And they will do just about anything but engage with the issue of our collective right to determine our own end-of-life choices. Although it was

Nancy who drew attention to the failings in Queensland law, the Beattie government could not attack her; this would be unacceptable. Better, they thought, to target me.

After Nancy died, it wasn't long before the Queensland police embarked on the lengthy and expensive investigation that led to simultaneous police raids across three states in search of computers, documents and videotape associated with Nancy. Early one morning several squad cars screeched down my driveway in Darwin. I was greeted by plain-clothed officers in sunglasses, bolt-cutters in hand. It was just like in the movies. The only thing was that, being in Darwin, the police were overly enthusiastic in the execution of their search warrant, seizing a great deal more material than the warrant permitted. This led to a successful legal action against the Queensland government and the police commissioner, Bob Atkinson, by our lawyers, led by John Tippett QC. In the wash-up, the Queensland government was forced to pay our considerable legal costs, which came in at around $40 000. Nice work, I thought.

As is increasingly the case in Australia, Brisbane was, and is, a one-newspaper town, with Rupert Murdoch at the wheel. Given Nancy lived on the Gold Coast, her story was always destined to be covered first and most extensively by the local media, which in southeast Queensland means the *Gold Coast Bulletin* and the more widely read state paper, *The Courier Mail*, also owned by Murdoch. While he has never, to my knowledge, expressed an opinion one way or the other about voluntary euthanasia, senior journalists working in his flagship publications certainly have. *The Australian* led the attack in the wake of Nancy's death.

Another memorable incident involved the Melbourne *Age*'s health reporter, Julia Medew—who prior to, and since, has produced some excellent front-page journalism about voluntary euthanasia.[5] Under the Freedom of Information legislation, in 2011, Medew obtained data from the Victorian

Institute of Forensic Medicine. The data showed that fifty-one people in Australia had died of Nembutal overdoses in the ten years to 2010. Of these deaths, thirty-two (63 per cent) were of people aged over fifty years. However, six were aged twenty to twenty-nine years, with a further eight aged thirty to thirty-nine years. Medew's article opened with the broadside 'Australians in their 20s and 30s are killing themselves with the drug that controversial euthanasia advocate, Dr Philip Nitschke, has promoted as the "peaceful pill"', using the headline 'Euthanasia Drug Snares Young Australians'.[6]

Public reaction to the article was swift. I was accused of being irresponsible, reckless and downright dangerous. But this was unfair—at Exit we take every possible caution to prevent young people from getting information that would enable them to obtain Nembutal; we also know that young people don't attend Exit workshops. As to whether young people might buy printed copies of our banned *Peaceful Pill Handbook* from Amazon in the US and import them illegally, or access the online version, both of which provide this information, we don't know. However, another in-built safeguard is automatic. Acquiring Nembutal is a time-consuming and expensive process that does not lend itself to rash, spur-of-the-moment actions. But, with Medew's *Age* article, the damage was quickly done and the anti-euthanasia movement around the world immediately began using it as evidence of their long-held position that I should be prosecuted.[7]

It was not until five weeks after the article appeared that *The Age* ran a letter to the editor about the way the statistics had been reported. It came from the Head of the Victorian Institute of Forensic Medicine, Professor Joan Ozanne-Smith, who wrote:

> Subsequent analysis of the data shows at least nine of the 14 individuals aged under 40 who died from pentobarbitone toxicity worked in a veterinary or

animal laboratory environment … thus these people
may have had knowledge of the drug and/or process to
it from their work experience or workplace.

She continued:

We do not think the data supports the view that younger
people are generally accessing Nembutal/pentobarbitone
via euthanasia information.

Unfortunately, this was too little too late. *The Age* refused to
publish my letter to the editor, my only available right-of-reply.

There have been plenty of other examples of stories
being written about me where my version of events was never
going to get a fair run. The prime example of this concerned
the case of the 2008 death of West Australian psychiatric
patient, Erin Berg.

Erin was an occupational therapist in Perth, one of four
sisters, the other three of whom were social workers. Erin
was the only one of them with children, having had four by
the age of thirty-nine. She also had post-natal depression, and
had separated from her husband, Norman, before her fourth
child, Elizabeth, was born. Following this birth she suffered
from post-natal depression of such severity that she was cer-
tified and hospitalised as an involuntary patient.

On 21 April 2008, after six weeks in the Mother and Baby
Unit at King Edward Memorial Hospital for Women, Erin was
discharged by the Mental Health Review Board on the condition that she be monitored by the Fremantle Mental Health
Unit. Three weeks later, after securing permission for a 'short
holiday down south', she visited her ex-husband, Norman,
and handed baby Elizabeth over to him. Twelve hours later
she flew out of Australia for Mexico. Norman would later
acknowledge in an ABC radio documentary that Erin had
told him she was off to Los Angeles, although she denied she

was going to Tijuana. He even suggested to her that if she was planning on killing herself in Tijuana, to 'make sure you've got a will'.[8] And so it was that Erin Berg went to Tijuana with her husband's full knowledge. There, she allegedly purchased and drank Nembutal in a sleazy hotel room, but failed to die. When the news reached Australia, her sisters, in an understandable panic, boarded the next flight to LA. On arriving in Tijuana, they found Erin comatose in the Hospital General de Tijuana. She died five days later.

Before they left Australia, the Mother and Baby Unit at King Edward informed Erin's sisters that they had found a record of her having borrowed *Killing Me Softly* from the local library. The accusations flew, with *The Australian* journalist Victoria Laurie acting as the sisters' mouthpiece.[9] Laurie rang and interviewed me at length, laying out the sister's allegations. My answers were given little attention in the *Weekend Australian* piece that followed. I can now finally address that.

Accusation:
'While Nitschke stated his book was "not a how-to-die manual", the Doyle sisters would later argue that Erin had viewed it precisely in those terms.'

My response:
Of the 88 000 odd words that make up *Killing Me Softly*, a single sentence makes mention of Mexico as a source for Nembutal. 'Its availability in countries like Mexico and Indonesia has been investigated by Exit ...'

Accusation:
'How could Philip Nitschke have made such statements about a so-called "reliable" death?'

My response:
With no autopsy, no one knows what Erin did. Did she take a gulp from a bottle of Nembutal and vomit it up (given her sister reported her hotel room smelling of vomit)?[10] Did she die of alcohol poisoning? We will never know, no autopsy was ever done. Suspicion and hysteria are no substitute for scientific analysis.

Accusation:
'Another rude shock would confront the women in Mexico. They discovered that Tijuana, a border town between Mexico and the US, is a drug-trafficking capital where violence erupts daily … No such dangers were explained in Nitschke's books or on his website, even though he had visited Tijuana several times …'

My response:
As Victoria Laurie's article reached fever pitch, so I became accused of all manner of sins. In a book that does not discuss Tijuana, I should somehow have warned readers of the dangers to tourists in Tijuana?

Accusation:
'Nitschke's book didn't mention that Mexican law prohibits doctors from ceasing treatment, even in the event of no brain function …'

My response:
Why would I discuss the laws concerning medical treatment in Mexico?

Accusation:
'[Erin's sister's] partner, Noela, was so furious at their dilemma she fired off an email to Nitschke's Darwin-based organisation, Exit International. "I am truly horrified at the information you make so freely available on your internet and also in Nitschke-published

books, especially *Killing Me Softly*," she wrote. "You have a massive responsibility to ensure your message gets to the right people and is not reinterpreted by people who are sad, isolated or mentally ill.'"

My response:

This last accusation is perhaps the point that irks me most. Erin Berg did make contact with Exit on the 13th December 2007. How do I know? Because Exit's invaluable database tells me so. It tells me also that Erin tried to lie her way into Exit membership, only to be turned down by our nurse. Of course, there are plenty of women in their late thirties who have cervical cancer. But Erin was not one of them. In the course of trying to talk her way into Exit, Erin disclosed that she had had five breakdowns over the past ten years and that one breakdown had lasted for a continuous two years. As a result Erin was advised to contact WA psychiatric services and to let her family know of her pain and suffering. She was told in no uncertain terms that Exit was not for her, she could not attend a workshop and there was no way we could help her.

I'm not sure what more I could or should have done, but to Victoria Laurie and the *Weekend Australian*, that didn't matter. Nothing was going to get in the way of her story.

My relationship with journalists (and their editors and producers) spans the gamut of human emotion. There are those I really like and some I see socially. There are others who simply don't engage with me or with voluntary euthanasia (sometimes, it seems, one is synonymous with the other). And there are those whose gigs I know I'll probably never get, and I'll never know why. *Q&A*, hosted by Tony Jones on ABC television, and Alan Jones and Roy Hadley on Sydney's 2GB are a few that spring to mind.

My interview with CNN's Connie Chung in the San Diego studio, while she was at HQ in New York, was memorable for several reasons. With an audience in the millions, a grab on prime-time CNN is important in anyone's language. But it was a particularly nasty exchange, one that could hardly be called an interview. Connie simply hammered me, interrupting at every point, suggesting that I had exploited a vulnerable and lonely Lisette Nigot when I agreed to help her die.

Her San Diego producer must have taken pity on this hapless Australian who had arrived in the US amid such controversy (the press were aware that the prototype carbon monoxide generator I had designed and had planned to display in San Diego had been confiscated by Customs as I was leaving Australia). On my way out the studio door, the producer called me aside and said, 'You might be interested in this.' 'This' was the recording of the NYC producer's feed. The feed is the invisible audio line that goes into the presenter's ear, and feeds questions and angles as an interview progresses. If you look carefully, you can see the discreetly positioned, curly translucent wire as its snakes out of a presenter's collar.

So, accompanying Connie's interview, was the goading from the production sidelines. 'You've got him, Connie, go for the kill, you've got him!' screamed the anonymous voice. And kill, Connie did. It seems that a sensible conversation about one's right to determine when and how one dies is beyond some media people's ability. I'm sure I'm not alone in finding such an approach insulting, even if the dramatics make for interesting, if fleeting, television.

While Connie's approach to our interview that night was neither fair nor professional, she is hardly alone. In Australia, commentators such as Neil Mitchell (on Melbourne radio station 3AW), and Murdoch-stable stalwarts Andrew Bolt and David Penberthy often take the same path. While Bolt is well-known for his rantings—and his habit of adopting a contrary opinion, seemingly merely for the sake of generating controversy and a pay packet—Penberthy and his offsider Tory Shepherd are a little more insidious.

Over the past decade, Penberthy has been unable to engage in the voluntary euthanasia issue without side-swiping me over whatever takes his fancy. Is it my 'gravestone toothy smile'? Is it my 'trademark hangdog expression'? When my photograph is used to illustrate his savage opinion pieces with the caption, 'Would you be seen dead in this shirt?' one has to wonder at a journalist who can't help but attack my physical appearance. One is never given a chance to answer. Inevitably these attacks are from people I have no respect for, but they do damage. My standard response: You can call me names and criticise my appearance—none of that matters. What is important are the ideas—try at least to get the ideas right. The debate over voluntary euthanasia can be vicious. There is a lot at stake and there are some big egos at play, especially in the case of journalists who seem to think that I have gained too a high profile, too easily and for too long. And on occasions, it has been members of the alternative online press who have come to my rescue, a good example of which was the September 2012 article by Andrew Crook 'Fight over Clem Jones bequest splits right-to-die movement'.

While working with the media can be a balancing act, there are many occasions where journalists are supportive of me and the voluntary euthanasia issue. Indeed, in some interviews I have questions put to me in such a positive way that all I need do is agree. While such moments might not amount to hard-hitting journalism, I am grateful for the breaks they provide. Prominent among such media figures are television personality Kerri-Anne Kennerley; the 'human headline', Derryn Hinch (formerly of 3AW Melbourne); the delightful Reverend Bill Crews (2GB Sydney); Howard Sattler (6PR Perth); John Laws; and former Country Liberal

Party minister Daryl Manzie on Territory FM radio in Darwin.

In the social-media sphere, similar instances of goodwill abound. The reactions on my Facebook page and to my tweets are as heartening as they are immediate. It is nice to know there are others of like mind, that my message is on target, and that I am not alone. But the blogging and twitterspheres have also brought out the mad and the downright dangerous, particularly amongst the fundamentalist Christians.

In Australia, the emergence in recent years of Christian activist and Democratic Labor Party hopeful Paul Russell and his 'HOPE' anti-euthanasia group has not only led to a proliferation of skewed blog headlines, but also to an attack on my medical registration. A debate with Russell at the Liberal Club at the University of Adelaide in mid 2012 produced the blog headline 'Euthanasia Campaigner Philip Nitschke Meets His Match in Debate'. No one who attended thought that, but his blog on the event was immediately repeated and re-repeated throughout the global network of church and fundamentalist anti-euthanasia websites.

While he might be a polite, smiling and even warm-hearted opponent, Russell's ruthless determination to have me deregistered as a doctor is unabating. That he is a former employee in the Office of Family and Life in the Catholic Church in Adelaide, as well as holding the DLP's number one Senate spot in the 2010 federal election, gives him ready access to several mainstream journalists, only too keen to push their own ideological bandwagons. And so it was that I learned about the launching of a second enquiry by the Australian Medical Board (AHPRA) into my fitness to practise medicine, not in a letter from the investigating authority, but rather from the senior political journalist of *The Australian* and Catholic hardliner, Dennis Shanahan. Dennis rang to inform me that his 'reliable sources' had told him of the

decision by the Medical Board to act on a complaint by Paul
Russell. His article, 'Nitschke Accused of Gas Import Scam'
would appear as an exclusive in the national press the following day. It was another week before I finally received formal
notification from AHPRA. Yes, a second investigation in
regard to my being a 'fit and proper' person to hold medical
registration had been launched. The reason? My involvement with Max Dog Brewing nitrogen cylinders. That
Shanahan knew of AHPRA's investigation before I did is
farcical. Of course, journalists will jump at the whiff of blood
and go for any headline. Interestingly, the same news story
produced a second, much friendlier headline, 'Nitschke May
Lose His Medical Licence Over Beer' in the NT News the
following day.[11]

Internationally, the anti-euthanasia internet campaign is
led by a number of zealots. Canadian pro-life activist Alex
Schadenberg is one. His parents are known in Canada as
pro-life pioneers and his blog shows a fixation on my activities
and those of Exit. Schadenberg, his American anti-euthanasia
counterpart Wesley J. Smith, and their UK equivalent, expat
New Zealander Peter Saunders use the new media relentlessly,
spreading the lies and half truths that have grown up over the
years. If I believed half of what they wrote, I'd be scared of me
too. However, truth is commonly the first casualty in debates
where religious fundamentalists are involved. Just ask the
feminists in the pro-choice/abortion debate.

When I look back on my interaction with the media,
it is Max Bell and Murray McLaughlin's ABC Four Corners
episode 'Road to Nowhere' that I come back to time and
time again. When surgeon Jon Wardill saw Max's suffering
on the ABC, he broke ranks with the medical establishment.
This was activist journalism at its best, whether McLaughlin
intended it to be or not.

Allen Ginsberg once famously noted 'whoever controls
the media … controls the culture', and so it is. I can forgive

the media much when it makes good things happen; when minds are prised open and democracy begins to work. Media coverage is pivotal to social change and my supping at the devil's table seems the necessary price to pay.

FIFTEEN

Censorship

The only valid censorship of ideas is the right of people not to listen.

Tom Smothers

Withholding information from people who need it has always annoyed me. It was the reason for my anger when I wasn't allowed to see or respond to the letter that was so critical of me when I took up my rangering job. Censorship offends one's sense of fair play and strikes at the heart of free speech. Over the past decade I've watched with dismay as censorship continues to rear its ugly head.

The censorship of euthanasia has taken many forms. Parliament has introduced laws and regulations to prevent elderly Australians from accessing the end-of-life information they want. This has seen the banning of the *Peaceful Pill Handbook*, the banning of a television commercial that Exit commissioned, and the near banning of an advertising bill-board. The Queensland Government even once sent an inspector to a workshop I was holding at the Brisbane City Library in order to ensure that a three-minute film made for Exit by Steve Hopes (*Do It Yourself with Betty*) about how to make an Exit bag would not be shown to the assembled audience of fifty or so octogenarians. The reason? The film had not been classified by the Office of Film and Literature Classification and may be 'objectionable'.

Internationally, YouTube has responded to complaints (who knows by whom or how many) to remove some of Exit's videos, including *Do It Yourself with Betty*. This quirky 2009 film featured retired nurse-educator Betty Peters OAM, who describes the steps involved in the home manufacture of an Exit bag. Once posted on YouTube.com, the comic and cleverly tongue-in-cheek *Betty* became an instant hit, rocketing up the rankings to become the most viewed video about voluntary euthanasia. For two years, nothing happened. Then, without warning, we were contacted by YouTube and told to remove the video, or we would have all of our YouTube films (about fifteen were running at that time) taken down. YouTube accused Exit of breaching its community standard guidelines. Given the questionable material released daily on YouTube, my initial thought was, *That's quite an achievement. How could anyone offend YouTube's standards?* I often comment at Exit meetings that, given the rubbish on YouTube, it takes some doing to offend them. Since that time someone unknown to me has ripped off the *Betty* video and reposted it back on YouTube under the title 'How to make an Exit bag'. While I'd normally complain about having my intellectual property stolen, this is one time I'm happy to let the matter go through to the keeper.[1]

Another instance of censorship internationally was PayPal's decision in mid 2012 to cancel Exit's account. Overnight I found that our account with PayPal had been frozen and several thousand dollars retained by them for six months. Google, too, has long had issues with sponsored ads mentioning the word 'euthanasia', arguing that voluntary euthanasia equates to the incitement of violence and is therefore unacceptable.

Other surreptitious acts aimed at stifling my words and damaging my reputation include hostile alterations to

Wikipedia entries related to me and the tagging of Exit videos by pro-life groups (to enable, for example, unrelated pro-life videos to play immediately after the our films). Such attacks are unrelenting, often coming from expected quarters and occasionally from some quite unexpected places, both within Australia and overseas.

The banning of *The Peaceful Pill Handbook* in early 2007 was not the first instance of the Australian Government censoring my voluntary euthanasia work, although it has been the most enduring. This practical guidebook took many years to write and came about primarily because I became unable to keep up with the demand for practical end-of-life information. Every day questions would arrive by letter, email, fax and phone. 'How can I store my Mexican Nembutal so it will be okay in ten years?' 'I've got asthma, can I still use an Exit bag with nitrogen?' And so on. There was no way of answering so many individual questions, so many times over. The logical solution was a mass-market paperback. Even as the project took shape, the politically hostile climate in Australia suggested that a book of this nature would need to be published elsewhere. With its constitutional protection of free speech, the United States was the obvious place to do it. But let me backtrack.

The first time I felt the heavy hand of censorship being applied to the euthanasia issue was in 2001. This was following an especially well-attended series of Exit workshops. Wesley J. Smith—one of several Americans who have become key adversaries over the years—made a speaking visit to Australia that year. After an interview in *The Australian* newspaper, Catholic journalist Dennis Shanahan ran a front-page story claiming that elderly Australians were importing custom-made plastic Exit bags from a Canadian activist by the name of Evelyn Martens.[2] Dennis, who strongly opposes voluntary euthanasia, accused me of telling people that plastic bags could be used for a peaceful hypoxic (low-oxygen) death. He called the process a grim suffocation (which it's not).[3] However, the article had its desired effect. The very next day, 21 August 2001, the Howard government's Justice and Customs Minister, Chris Ellison, called for an urgent report from Customs to determine whether there were grounds to prevent the importation of plastic bags into Australia. While the ministerial directive seemed bizarre, it didn't stop there. Ellison didn't only want the physical items, the plastic bags, seized, he also wanted to intercept 'information' about them. He wanted to outlaw all information that might explain what they did and why.

On 5 September 2002, Senator Ellison got his way. On that day, the *Customs Act* was quietly amended to prohibit the import or export of items associated with ending one's life and, more importantly, *information* about these items. Like most Australians I was unaware of this important change. Indeed, it was not until I was leaving the country in early January 2003, and got dragged out of the boarding queue at Tullamarine Airport, that the Minister's intentions really hit home.

Usually, as you go through Customs and Immigration, they scan your passport, say a few words and on you go to your waiting flight. But on this occasion, I was not waved on. Instead, I was taken aside to a small room where I found the contents of my suitcases spread out before me.

'We have found items in your luggage that breach the Australian *Customs Act*.'

I was perplexed.

He went on, 'We have found printed material,' they said, holding up some pieces of paper. 'What are these?' one of them asked, holding up some PVC tubing.

I said, 'I'm on my way to a right-to-die conference in San Diego.'

There was to be no negotiation. While I was eventually allowed through, my 'COGen' (a carbon-monoxide generator) and the accompanying instruction sheets were retained by the officer. When I asked where such authority came from, the reply was: 'It's a change to the Act. Here's a copy of it; read it if you like, and see your lawyers.'

News of the airport incident reached Los Angeles before I did, and the cameras were waiting. The American media seemed perplexed: end-of-life information confiscated— how bad must it have been? 'You wouldn't have that problem here,' was the common comment. I had two weeks to reflect on the issue, and wondered, *What's happening to my country?* On my return to Australia, I was again taken out of the queue and my bags searched, and more printed material was removed. Australia was joining the long list of infamous regimes that censor the written word.

And the censoring of information about voluntary euthanasia is not solely the domain of politicians. When Janine Hosking's feature documentary *Mademoiselle and the Doctor* was scheduled to be shown on the *Compass* program on ABC television in 2005, presenter Geraldine Doogue took it upon herself to personally object. Doogue demanded that a ninety-second segment of the film be removed. This was the scene where Lisette Nigot (Mademoiselle) discusses why she will not use an Exit bag to take her own life. Although the film had been examined and approved by ABC lawyers prior to screening, Doogue issued a statement saying the segment 'breached our editorial codes and responsibility as a public broadcaster' and could not, therefore, be screened. When the incident was examined on the ABC's *Media Watch* program, Janine Hosking expressed her frustration, adding that the film had become a 'study guide shown to senior secondary school students' throughout Australia.[4]

Although the changes to the *Customs Act* were cause for concern, I was not overly worried. In the back of my mind was the thought that airport searches for restricted information were never going to be effective. After all, I could just shift the paper version of the information onto USB drive. That would fool the Customs officers. And besides, why bother even taking it with me when I could just as easily load it onto the internet before my departure. Indeed, my smug response when asked about the *Customs Act* amendments was, 'Fine; if that's the way the government wants it, we'll just put the material on the internet.'

My complacency was, however, to be short lived. I soon heard of another piece of proposed legislation; the *Suicide-Related Materials Offences Act*. This Act amends the *Commonwealth Criminal Code*, and makes it a crime to use a 'carriage service' (i.e. the internet) to send or receive suicide-related material. In other words, it prohibits the use of the internet, email, fax and telephone to discuss the practical aspects of voluntary euthanasia.

In the months prior to this legislation being brought before the federal parliament, a Senate inquiry was held. I put in a submission opposing it, and travelled to Canberra to appear at the public hearings. The Greens and the Democrats opposed the law at both the inquiry level and in parliament, but to no avail. In September 2006, the amendment was passed with the full support of the major parties. And so in Australia it is now against the law to pick up the telephone and talk to your brother or sister, or anyone else for that matter, about the possibility of ending one's life and how to go about it. Like changes to the *Customs Act* before it, most Australians remain blissfully unaware of what their government has done.

The publication of *The Peaceful Pill Handbook* in the US, in September 2006, marked an important turning point in our attempt to insulate Exit's activities from Australian Government interference. From our new operating base in Michigan, headed by my old friend Neal Nicol, the one-time assistant of Dr Jack Kevorkian, the fledgling US arm of Exit International was born. From day one, the *Handbook* took off and now sells widely around the world, satisfying the growing needs of elderly people wanting to be informed about their practical end-of-life choices.

The book was launched by Derek Humphry in Toronto at the World Federation Right to Die Societies annual conference. Derek's landmark book *Final Exit* had been published more than a decade earlier and, as I write in the dedication of *The Peaceful Pill Handbook*, Derek had 'paved the way'. At the launch, there was no indication of problems associated with publishing a book of this nature. However, it was not long until big problems would emerge. After the conference, we planned to bring some forty copies of the new book back to Australia for Exit members. As Fiona and I were travelling on to Mexico to undertake some Nembutal R&D, Exit's Gold Coast Coordinator, Elaine Arch-Rowe, was flying straight back to Brisbane. It made sense that she take the copies with her. No one expected there to be an issue. The US-published book had its own ISBN number, was freely selling in bookshops, and was available on Amazon. But Australian Customs had other ideas.

At Brisbane Airport, Elaine's suitcase was seized by Customs and all forty books confiscated. Again the legislation cited was the *Customs Act*. Crazy, but not unheard of. (Some eighty years earlier in 1930, Australian Customs had seized copies of Norman Lindsay's banned booked *Redheap*, about a fictitious Australian country town. The ban on this book would not be overturned in Australia until 1958, despite selling freely around the world in the intervening twenty–eight–year period.) At this point, I thought, *All right, let's be sensible and apply to have the book formally classified. Let's test its right to be distributed in Australia. If that's successful, we'll be able to publish without the need to import.*

After going through the paperwork and paying the (significant) fee, we submitted the book to the Office of Film and Literature Classification for formal classification in October 2006. While I wasn't very hopeful, we were at least playing by the rules. In December, we received a very pleasant surprise: 'Restricted R18' classification. This meant that anyone over eighteen years could legally buy *The Peaceful*

Pill Handbook, but it would need to be sold in plain paper wrapping, and carry the required R18 classification logo on the front cover. Just like hardcore porn, it would need to be stored under a store's counter, rather than on open display. We could live with these conditions. We were thrilled. An initial print run of 5000 soon sold out. But the Howard government was not done yet. Within four weeks of being granted the R18 classification, I got a phone call from *The Australian*'s top sleuth, Dennis Shanahan. I was in the US at the time but I remember the call well. Dennis wanted comment on how I felt about Federal Attorney-General Philip Ruddock's decision to appeal the judgment of the independent Office of Film and Literature Classification. This was the first I knew that Ruddock was escalating the matter. He was demanding that the decision of the Classification Review Board be reviewed. The co-initiator of the appeal was Right to Life Australia. The government waived Right to Life's application fees.

We attended this new hearing in Sydney the following month. Although we were lucky to be represented by the wonderful folk at the Public Interest Advocacy Centre, we were not optimistic. Other parties present included the New South Wales Council for Civil Liberties, along with author and activist Frank Moorhouse. Right to Life was represented by its own lawyers, and lawyers from the Attorney-General's department were there in force. No one was surprised when the review decision went against us: the *Handbook*'s previous R18 classification was overturned and replaced by an RC rating (refused classification). This meant our book would be banned—the first Australian book to be banned in this country in thirty-five years! Interestingly, the Attorney-General's department gave evidence 'in camera', so we never heard what they had to say. Even though our barrister, Simeon Beckett, complained, suggesting a lack of natural justice, his laments fell on deaf ears.

If Philip Ruddock suspected that Exit lacked the funds needed to take the matter further in the Federal Court, he was right. It was too big a risk in that political climate. Instead, as authors and publishers, we were forced to run around, collecting the books from Australian bookshop shelves so they could be destroyed. The Managing Director of the Australian Christian Lobby, Jim Wallace, issued a press release at the time congratulating Right to Life on its 'win in having Nitschke's book banned'. While it may have been clear who was driving the government's agenda, what was more alarming was its willingness to comply.

In March 2007 we held a public bonfire in front of old Parliament House in Canberra, as part of our Day of Shame activities. We burnt hundreds of copies of the book. It seemed a fitting time for such a barbarous act. The Day of Shame wasn't a celebration either. It was a two-day event held by Exit to mark the tenth anniversary of the overturning of the ROTI Act by the Kevin Andrews Act. Among the events were a march through Canberra and a dinner at the National Museum that was hosted by Phillip Adams. At Parliament House, Exit members presented politicians from the Greens, Democrats and Labor parties with twenty-five 'Condolence Books'. These books contained messages from thousands of voluntary euthanasia supporters all over Australia, calling on Parliament to rescind the Andrews Act. The ABC's *Four Corners* covered the Day of Shame protest in a program called 'Final Call'.[5] Burning the books was something from the Dark Ages, especially since the *Handbook* at this stage was selling freely and openly in almost all other western countries.

The reasons given for banning the book were laughable. Chief among them was the allegation that the *Handbook* 'instructs in matters of crime'; that is, it tells you how you might synthesise end-of-life drugs. At the hearings, we had pointed out that *Vogel's Textbook of Practical Organic Chemistry* does exactly the same thing. Indeed, that is where much of our knowledge had come from. The board's reply was terse. Our book was different because it explained the process in 'accessible language'. They were saying, in effect, that it is all right for a student of organic chemistry to synthesise barbiturates, but it's not all right to describe it in simple language that everyone else can understand.

Political interference such as the Minister's decision to appeal the judgment of the Office of Film and Literature Classification showed once again the power certain pressure groups have to corrupt the legitimate processes of civil society. Many of us found Minister Ruddock's actions disgusting, as he allowed ideology and personal prejudice to influence the due process of an 'independent' government body.

Around the same time, a similar battle opened up over the Tasman. As we planned a New Zealand book launch and workshop tour, the Society for the Protection of Community Standards mobilised, lobbying the New Zealand Government. They urged that our now-banned Australian book be kept from their shores. Here, though, we had a partial victory. The newly appointed Chief Censor of New Zealand, Bill Hastings, resisted. After some months of deliberation, a compromise was reached. If we would remove (or black-out) around thirty offending paragraphs, the book would be cleared for New Zealand publication. This was unexpected, and even felt like a win. One of my clear memories of that time was meeting Bill in his office, high above Wellington, to receive the decision. Bill was keen for his staff to take a photograph of the two of us to record the event. I was pleased to agree.

By the beginning of 2007, I felt jaded by the whole *Peaceful Pill Handbook* censorship affair. It seemed every move we made, the government would make a counter-move, in a David and Goliath battle. It was becoming clear; we needed to use the internet and publish in an overseas jurisdiction— out of reach of the long arm of the persecutory Australian authorities. Via Exit's US publishing company, the online

Peaceful Pill eHandbook was launched in London in October 2008. This was not simply the print-format book taken online. After searching the world for innovative methods of publishing, we settled on a British company, Yudu, who marketed a publishing platform that included videos and audio, as well as text, making the book a multi-media experience. The online format also allows hyperlinks to other websites, so a huge amount of information and related background detail is available. Because republication is at the click of a button, revised and upgraded information can be made available on an ongoing basis, while inaccurate or obsolete content is discarded. As the *eHandbook* is published in the US, it is not subject to Australian law, although this does make me wonder about the efficacy of Australia's *Suicide-Related Material Offences Act*.

Finally, in 2008, we felt that we were on the front foot and that the battle had been won. But then the government opened up a new front. Within a month of the online *eHandbook*'s release, the Labor Minister for Communications, Senator Stephen Conroy, announced a proposal for mandatory internet filtering by Internet Service Providers, a so-called 'clean feed'. While the original idea for such a filter had come from Kim Beazley when he was Labor Opposition Leader, its claimed objectives were the same—to protect the nation's children from child pornography.

In the period leading up to the proposed legislation, the government compiled a secret blacklist of over a thousand websites that would be banned once the law was passed and suitable filtering technology implemented. While I had my suspicions, it wasn't until WikiLeaks published the blacklist in March 2009 that I discovered that *The Peaceful Pill eHandbook* website (*www.peacefulpill.com*) was included. This was the only voluntary euthanasia site to be targeted. (Interestingly, as soon as WikiLeaks published the government's secret list, it found itself added to the same blacklist.) At this point, it became clear that the blacklist was also about more than just child pornography, or even porn in general. The government had another agenda. The blacklist allowed the Minister to use his discretion to ban almost any website he wanted, and there would be no system of appeal. I was left wondering if anyone cared that Australia was heading down the same censorship route as the dictatorships and theocracies of such countries as North Korea, the United Arab Emirates, Iran and China.

Throughout 2009 and 2010 the question of the mandatory filter and the blacklist was increasingly discussed in the media, and at public debates and forums. In *The Sydney Morning Herald*, conservative commentator Michael Duffy (himself a voluntary euthanasia supporter) wrote a column titled 'Web filtering pulls plug on euthanasia debate'.[6] Speaking about his article at a Politics in the Pub night in Sydney soon after, Duffy asked rhetorically 'What do these three sites have in common: *www.pantyass.com*, *www.peacefulpill.com* and *www.pickyourperversion.com*?' Of course, these are sequential 'P' listings from the websites Senator Conroy was planning to ban. There was my book, sandwiched between the porn and titillation.

But there is often a light side to such darkness; there has to be. During the 2010 National Science Festival in Canberra, Fiona and I were invited by Erica Ryan, the Manager of Collections at the National Library, to visit the underground storage vaults. I jumped at the chance, as this secure area is where the nation's banned books and other 'dangerous' printed materials are housed. The vaults are in the basement, behind thick steel doors and under lock and key—a maximum-security prison for books. With lock after lock finally opened, we were shown my little book, wedged in between titles such as *Busty Broads* and *Tales of Tom Thumb*. With a mischievous look, Erica took the book from the shelf and suggested we might like to autograph the copy. Fiona marked the occasion with a photograph. I had to laugh. The only other place *The Peaceful Pill Handbook* is legally held in Australia is Parliament House Library in Canberra.

At a grassroots level, Exit responded to the threat of the clean feed by introducing our elderly members to concepts such as 'virtual private networks' and 'internet tunnels', which are technological means of getting around an internet filter. We placed our regular information workshop program on hold and hastily convened alternative meetings that focused on ways to subvert government censorship. With expertise from the twenty-something geeks of the Pirate Party, we held hacking meetings on the east coast of Australia. It was wonderful to see our senior citizens arriving with laptops and wi-fi modems in hand, ready to learn how to keep their internet access free from government interference. After all, if their grandchildren could hack through their schools' firewalls, surely they could also learn such skills? ABC television's *Four Corners* program covered Exit's response to the government's censorship plans in a report by Quentin McDermott titled: 'Access Denied'.[7]

In 2010 the ongoing war on censorship recommenced when we attempted to air a pro-choice euthanasia television commercial. A billboard was planned to be unveiled not long after. While the commercial was banned outright, the billboard did eventually go up on the Hume Highway, south of Sydney.

In July that year, the ABC's comedy program based around the ad industry, *The Gruen Transfer*, featured 'compulsory euthanasia for the over 80s' as part of their Pitch segment. The Pitch is where two ad agencies each make a television commercial that seeks to sell the impossible. Among the more infamous pitches have been those selling child labour and the banning of all religion. Sydney agency The Works, led by Kevin Macmillan, won the euthanasia pitch with a delightful and innovative ad. At the time, Exit had come into a sizeable bequest. We contacted Kevin with a view to entering the advertising fray. Three months later, the 'Exit Choices' television commercial was completed.

The advertisement shows a man in his pyjamas sitting on the edge of his bed, talking about the choices he's made through his life: 'Life's all about choices. Like I chose to go to uni and study engineering.' The ad ends with the man asking why he isn't allowed to decide to end his suffering from cancer, which, as he states, he 'didn't choose to get'.[8] In Australia, all advertisements must be approved by the Commercials Advice process of a quasi-governmental body called 'Free TV Australia'. In the case of Exit's advertisement, approval was given, only to be suddenly withdrawn at the last moment.[9] No reason was provided. Free TV's counsel issued a statement saying that the commercial provided 'a realistic depiction of methods of suicide' and was thereby 'invariably unsuitable' for television. Of course, this was rubbish. The commercial showed nothing more than a man in his pyjamas sitting on an unmade bed talking about the decisions he had made in his life. His wife is in the frame behind him, a mug of coffee in her hand. No discussion on 'method', and no 'depiction'. With no appeal process, it seemed our $25 000 investment had been wasted.

While the commercial never ran in the Channel 7 late-night spot we purchased (luckily, we got our money back), *The Gruen Transfer* took a keen interest in the issue. The censorship of a commercial piqued their interest. In their last show for 2010, they had their panel critically examine the commercial on air. They then played it in its entirety. Thanks to *The Gruen Transfer*, the advertisement and the Exit message got out. What was particularly pleasing was that the commercial was seen by millions of TV viewers (not to mention those who have since seen it on YouTube). This was advertising space we could never have afforded. Sometimes censorship has a silver lining.

The TV commercial was followed by a billboard campaign. Inspired by the success of atheist groups in the UK

who had created controversy by purchasing space on the side
of double-decker buses for their secular mass media messages
('There's probably no god, now stop worrying and enjoy
your life'), our billboard plan was put into action. We kept the
message simple, with no graphics and no images—nothing
'objectionable'. The message: '85% of Australians support
Voluntary Euthenasia. Our Government doesn't. Make them
Listen.' We took this statistic from the October 2009 Newspoll
that had been published in *The Australian*, as we thought no
one could argue with it.[10] How wrong we were.

Within days, the Australian Advertising Standards Bureau
started receiving complaints.[11] Some requested anonymity
(which, apparently, is permissible), while other complainants
proudly named themselves. Andrea Callihanna wrote: 'I find
this billboard to be entirely offensive because it is advertising
and promoting activity which is illegal and fatal to anyone
who acts on it ie SUICIDE'. A Mrs Gresser wrote: 'Publicly
claiming that Australians support euthanasia is an attack on
the elderly and ill members of our society ...' Again, Exit
was forced to spend time defending its message. For once
though, the authorities agreed with us, and the complaints
were dismissed. Our billboard remained on view through to
November that year.

While these examples of censorship are writ large on
the public record, others are more discreet. The sudden cancellation of speaking engagements is a good example. One
memorable instance occurred when I received an invitation
in March 2009 to participate in a debate at the Oxford Union
in the UK. The Oxford Union prides itself on being the
world's most famous debating club, with a long and impressive
line-up of past speakers, from former US presidents, to rock
stars and royals. The invitation read: 'Our members would be
delighted to welcome the founder of an organisation like Exit
International to address our chamber ...', in other words, to
speak about voluntary euthanasia. I was excited at the prospect.

Five days later, a second email arrived, this time rescinding the offer. It read: 'I am afraid that we have encountered something of a problem as we have had great difficulty getting other speakers to agree to speak alongside Dr Nitschke … it is therefore with sadness that we feel obliged to retract our invitation.' I was left wondering what on earth was going on. Who did they have speaking next to me? The pope?

An Australian Associated Press wire report provided the explanation. Another speaker was to be Dr Michael Irwin. Irwin's hostility had been revealed back in 2009, with his public attacks in the British media about my 'irresponsibility' in holding UK Exit workshops. But it didn't really matter who the other speakers were, the result was the same: I was barred from speaking, so my ideas could never be aired. On looking into the issue, I found that I was only the third person in the entire 190-year history of the Oxford Union to have had their invitation withdrawn; the two others speakers were the Holocaust denier David Irving and John Tyndall, the far-right founder of the British National Party. Hardly the best company to be keeping. I was mildly amused when, in mid 2012, a grovelling second invitation arrived from John Lee, the new President of the Union, asking if they could 'redeem themselves by hosting you here finally at the Oxford Union'.[12] As if to add insult to injury, Mr Lee added: 'I have already chatted to our confirmed speakers on the proposition side, Dr Michael Irwin and Richard Ottaway MP, and they are happy to debate on the same side as you.' Too little, far too late. Whether or not Irwin had reversed his position, I really couldn't be bothered with him or the Oxford Union. I told them I'd think about, and then let it lapse.

Finally, some acts of censorship go far beyond hurt feelings and a bruised ego, and have significant financial ramifications, such as when PayPal cancelled Exit's long-standing account and froze our funds without warning in mid 2012. Their reason? Contravention of their 'Acceptable Use Policy'.

After a business relationship lasting almost six years, this about-turn came from nowhere, and there was no appeal process. The suspension occurred around the same time that I took part in a particularly hostile debate at the City Bible Forum in Sydney, and there was considerable criticism of me and Exit in the international anti-euthanasia blogs and websites. While the PayPal ban was probably a coincidence, experience has long taught me to be wary of the lengths opponents will go to silence what I have to say. Moral-issue politics is a dirty business, with few rules.

I don't expect that the censorship foot will come off our throats any time soon. I'd like to think that, in years to come, Australians will look back at government attempts to censor information on voluntary euthanasia and laugh, in the same way that younger generations now find it hard to believe that books such as *Lolita* by Vladimir Nabokov and the song 'Davy's Little Dingy' by the delightful American singer Ruth Wallis were ever banned.[13] While there are instances where control of the flow of information is necessary—say, in matters of terrorism and national security—the enthusiasm of governments to censor end-of-life choices knowledge is worrying. The rationale seems to be that if you keep people in the dark about death and dying, they will live longer and happier lives, sitting there smiling, well into their nineties.

Of course, quite the opposite is true. It is when you empower people with knowledge and restore choice that they live longer and happier lives. As difficult as my opponents may find it, knowledge brings comfort. Choice over when to die can be life-affirming. Unfortunately, this is a point that remains lost on most of the politicians of the nation. For this reason, I doubt there will be legislative change on the voluntary euthanasia issue any time soon. The irony is that, if asked, most elderly people will tell you that they don't have time to wait around.

SIXTEEN

Going global

He is one of the international euthanasia movement's rock stars, and despite his supposedly 'fringe' views, is always invited to the big international euthanasia conferences, and indeed, travels the world literally pitching his poison.

Wesley J. Smith, US anti-euthanasia activist

I've made more trips overseas as a voluntary euthanasia campaigner than I can count, usually, but not always, to English-speaking countries. During the time of ROTI, I underwent a baptism of fire, with an avalanche of speaking engagements coming my way. I found myself doing everything from addressing the Spanish Parliament, to being flown to London to appear as an expert witness in a BBC courtroom hypothetical. I've also undertaken a number of clandestine overseas visits, carrying out 'field research' in Mexico, Indonesia and elsewhere, in the ongoing search for over-the-counter Nembutal and other useful end-of-life drugs. During these trips, I've come to know the US–Mexican border region, with all its beauty and danger, quite well. Looking back, I've probably been lucky: walking unprotected into a compound in Denpasar, Indonesia, to pick up a bottle of illegal Nembutal, just so I could get a photo for the *Handbook*, or being rescued by a total stranger as I searched for a non-existent drug contact

in the more dangerous alleys of Varez, Mexico, were both
events I'd rather not repeat.

Despite this life of apparent shoe-string jetsetting, it was
not until October 2008 that I began running Exit workshops in other countries. The first London workshop was
planned to coincide with the launch of *The Peaceful Pill
eHandbook* at Conway Hall, home of the South Place Ethical
Society, which champions free speech. Two other workshops
were planned, in Brighton and Bournemouth. I had picked
the UK south coast on the advice of a Channel 7 journalist,
Mike Duffy. He'd spent many years living in the UK and
knew that this area—an English version of Australia's Gold
Coast, a place known also as 'God's waiting room'—had an
elderly demographic that would ideally suit the Exit message.
However, even before I landed, the two booked venues in
regional centres, nervous about growing media interest, cancelled our bookings. The London workshop went ahead, but
with only a handful of attendees, although Robin Mackenzie
from the Medicine and Ethics Department at the University
of Kent, and Neal Nicol, now our US publisher, did participate. With so few contacts in the UK, it was impossible to
find replacement venues for the regional centres at such
short notice. Instead, a follow-up visit in several months' time
was scheduled.

That initial visit to the UK was fraught from the time I
arrived. While I did expect some media interest in our activities and had actively courted it from Australia as a way of
promoting the workshops, and the usual complaints from
religious groups, I didn't expect the criticism that was levelled
at me from the local voluntary euthanasia society, Dignity in
Dying. This long-established group is one of the oldest and
wealthiest voluntary pro-euthanasia groups in the world,
with a corporate structure that employs a swag of adminis-
trators and media minders. Ever alert to the possibility of an

outside threat, they moved quickly to condemn the planned UK Exit workshop program.

My first media appearance on this 2008 trip was on the highly regarded *Today* program on BBC Radio 4, hosted by John Humphrys. However, instead of debating an expected Catholic Church spokesperson—as I was expecting—I found myself sparring with Dignity in Dying's CEO, Sarah Wootten. Here we were, both representing the voluntary euthanasia movement, and fighting among ourselves. Our opponents would have loved it. I made multiple media appearances with Sarah that day, and she always had the same message: that I was a dangerous and irresponsible doctor giving the elderly and seriously ill damaging information on how they might kill themselves. My workshops, she argued, were inciting people to suicide and, as such, were illegal and should be banned. There was no place, it seemed, for co-existence, for a two-pronged approach with Exit providing DIY options for those with an immediate need, and the longer term strategy of Dignity in Dying with its focus on changing British law. Like Debbie Purdy, Sarah argued that it was irresponsible for Exit to provide the rational elderly with practical end-of-life information. Rather, she insisted, the UK law needed to change to give doctors the right to select, and possibly help, end the life of the terminally ill. To Sarah, DIY death was an anathema, and on my subsequent 2009 UK visit, Dignity in Dying even went so far as to call for my deportation.

In retrospect, the behaviour of Dignity in Dying should not have been surprising. Back in 1998, when I was invited to London to donate the Deliverance Machine to the British Science Museum, this group boycotted the ceremony. The directors of the museum couldn't understand their hostility and neither could I. Over time, the cause for this antagonism has become a little clearer. With such organisations, their raison d'être is about legislative change that would bring about a medically mediated system to help the dying. DIY 'solutions' such as I was proposing in my workshops, require no change in the law, and all but eliminate the involvement of the medical profession. Dignity in Dying saw my approach as anarchic and dangerous, and ultimately one that would make their job of law reform even harder.

On the 2008 trip, there were several media encounters that stood out. I remember a particularly nasty incident where I was ambushed on gardener Alan Titchmarsh's popular afternoon program on ITV. The two others on the panel—one a doctor—were clearly hostile, perhaps not surprisingly. But what I was not expecting was the relentless bullying of Titchmarsh himself. As the panellists attacked, again arguing that my workshops were irresponsible and dangerous, Titchmarsh ensured I had no opportunity to respond. Every time I opened my mouth I was cut short, and the others given the stage. When it became obvious that I had been set up, I suggested, in the few words that I was given, that Alan might like to interview himself, but that I would no longer cooperate. As I came out of the studio, it was heartening to hear Fiona's voice coming from the main BBC foyer, shouting at Titchmarsh's producer, who was trying desperately to quieten her, that they should have been ashamed of themselves for treating me with such disrespect.

While these media battles were being fought, venue cancellations were threatening the whole workshop program. Suddenly there were last-minute cancellations of bookings that had been made months earlier. Excuses were sometimes provided, but not always. Those who did try to explain said they feared a backlash if the workshops proceeded, with possible violence or damage to the venue. I had no way of knowing if the threats were real, but last-minute cancellation of a venue is a very effective means of censorship. The chaos caused, with little or no time to locate or even publicise an alternative, effectively prevents the message from reaching an audience.

A win perhaps, for our opponents, but not completely. A frequent, but unexpected reaction was that some in the community were so incensed by this behaviour, which they saw as an attack on free speech, that they were moved to help by trying to find venues that could be used at a later date. Important ones identified were the Brighthelm Community Church in Brighton, under the tutelage of Reverend David Coleman, and Hamilton Hall Hotel in Bournemouth, which is a naturist resort for gay men. As well, the wonderful David Michael, formerly a councillor in Stroud in Gloucestershire, offered the local community hall as a venue. So, even though the first UK workshop program had been all but paralysed by controversy, seeds of hope were planted for a possible future visit.

The second visit to the UK took place a few months later and our meetings and workshops did take place, but only just. A new threat had emerged. At Heathrow, Fiona and I found ourselves ushered out of the queue at Immigration, and down into the labyrinth of underground corridors to a bare room and told we were being detained. The reason: they needed time to decide if I was a suitable person to be allowed into their country. Fiona could have gone on, but I'm glad she decided to stay. We waited while the officers examined news reports past and present, trying to identify grounds for entry or deportation. All of our luggage was with us and a great deal of attention was directed at a small plastic container with three hypodermic syringes, labelled 'Exit Nembutal Test Kit'. While there was nothing illegal about the kit—it had been developed for home testing of euthanasia drugs—they were clearly worried. Then the Immigration officers located a recent *Time* magazine article about the development of the kit, called 'Foolproofing suicide with euthanasia test kits'[1] and we were told we just had to wait while the decision was made.

To the Immigration officers' credit, while we weren't allowed to have a lawyer present in the interviews, we were given unfettered access to our mobile phones. The first call

I made was to Murray McLaughlin at the ABC in Darwin, telling him of the detention. Within minutes, the story was on the international newswire. I remember one Immigration officer coming into the holding room where we were waiting, muttering something like, 'This is particularly unhelpful.'

Our second call home was to our barrister in Sydney. We were lucky; she was out walking her dog with another lawyer friend, whose sister was married to London media lawyer Mark Stephens (who would go on to represent Julian Assange in one of his many court battles over extradition to Sweden). He contacted the Home Office, demanding answers, and also rang his friend Geoffrey Robertson QC, in case we needed backup. I'd crossed paths with Robertson years earlier, on his *Hypotheticals* television series. As word got round, other major media players got involved. Cole Morton at *The Guardian* contacted the Home Office to see if he could get access to me to complete a forthcoming profile piece. Journalists from *The Times, The Independent* and *The Observer* all weighed in, along with television and radio outlets throughout the UK and Europe. Nine hours after first setting foot in England, we were finally released, but with a strict ten days only on our visas. Bournemouth was beckoning, not only to hold the much delayed and rescheduled workshop, but also for the European launch of the prototype Nembutal test kit.

The publicity generated from being detained worked to our advantage. The launch of the Nembutal test kit was one of those mad days of back-to-back media interviews. The ABC's London bureau did an interview, as did ABC America, and other major networks from around the world. As well, Reuters and Associated Press were at the launch and took some iconic photos. No fewer than five media live-cross satellite vans were parked outside the innocuous little Hamilton Hall Hotel in Bournemouth. There were no death threats or violent protests, and owner John Bellamy said it was the most fun he'd had in years, as he kept the tea and biscuits coming for both workshop attendees and media.

Never underestimate the interest the media shows when a euthanasia gadget or device is involved; I'd seen this before with the development of the Deliverance Machine back in 1996. Now here it was again, this time focused on the homemade Nembutal test kit. It was a prototype, after all, and looked like it: a set of three syringes in a small plastic box from a two-dollar shop in Darwin. But it was treated as though it was a suicide kit itself, presumably because of the presence of the hypodermic syringes. Fiona would later say it was the closest she got to experiencing the paparazzi, given the blinding camera flashes shot off in her face every time she opened the hotel's front door.

From Bournemouth, we moved on to Brighton, but just to hold a public meeting; the idea of a workshop had proven too controversial for Brighthelm Church's management committee. Nevertheless, the church's goodwill was very welcome and allowed us to break the Brighton black ban. Then it was on to the neighbouring seaside town of Eastbourne and once again, more doors closed in our faces, more cancelled venues. Again we had to promise to return at a later date, to make it happen sometime in the future. (It would take another two visits to Eastbourne before a venue would finally stand firm. With the help of Kathy Beech, a local who had been incensed by the earlier cancellations, a meeting and workshop took place at the Eastbourne Riviera Hotel in November 2011.)

The Stroud and Glasgow workshops went ahead without a hitch. A few protestors at Stroud held a prayer meeting outside the hall, but it was clear from the crowd of more than a hundred attending that we were offering something they wanted. Clearly, not all of the UK was as reactionary, or as timid, as the southern seaside centres. The further north we went, the easier it became.

Attention now turned to North America. While I had visited the US and Canada regularly for conferences and NuTech gatherings etc., now was the time to take the next step and run our own set of workshops to showcase Exit initiatives. The job of publicising our 2009 trip was made much easier when the Vancouver Public Library cancelled our booking, alleging that an Exit meeting would breach section 241 (a) and (b) of the *Canadian Criminal Code*, and that I would be guilty of counselling, aiding and abetting suicide. It was ironic that, the same week, the library ordered multiple copies of *The Peaceful Pill Handbook* and requested urgent shipping, presumably in response to heightened public demand.

I was totally amazed: more censorship, and this time in North America. We began looking around to see if we could find someone to help, someone willing to challenge this discrimination. We didn't have to look far—the British Columbia Civil Liberties Association (BCCLA) soon came to our rescue. Led by the indefatigable David Eby and with full backing of its board, the BCCLA insisted that the library hold a special meeting to reconsider their decision. When that didn't work, the BCCLA convened a press conference with the founder of the Canadian Farewell Foundation, Russel Ogden, which I attended via Skype from Darwin. The association's support of Exit that day was admirable. And it was also very pleasing to see them lead the successful 2012 Dying with Dignity case in the British Columbia Supreme Court, which saw the ban on assisted suicide struck down.[2] This legal battle is ongoing.

Again we were saved by the public reaction to the Library's attempt to ban my talk, and almost immediately, the Vancouver Unitarian Church stepped forward to fill the void. The Vancouver workshop then went ahead, as planned, in front of a packed audience. The Unitarians would later continue this support by providing Exit with workshop venues in Toronto and Montreal. Other workshops on that tour were held in San Francisco, Bellingham and Anaheim in southern California. No security was ever needed, despite my concerns, even in gun-bearing America. While our small Bellingham gathering was picketed by a disproportionately large crowd of right-to-lifers, the much bigger San Francisco meeting attracted only a handful of wheelchair protestors, this time from the Disability Rights Education and Defense Fund.

When well-known activist Marilyn Golden managed to get her wheelchair wedged in the front door of the San Francisco Buddhist Centre, where the workshop was being held, Fiona was able to quietly dislodge her, in what she says became a battle of brute force. Luckily for us, no photographs were taken.

Over the years, I have experienced right-to-life protests on a number of occasions. Nelson, on New Zealand's South Island, is home to a Christian sect called Light of Christ Covenants Community. They reliably turn out with their placards and their children each time we visit. We also had a Christian youth group demonstrate with megaphones outside a Sydney conference Exit was holding at the YWCA. However, it was not until we held a workshop in Ireland that we felt the full impact of organised opposition.

To date, we have held two series of workshops in Dublin, both attracting large numbers of pro-life demonstrators. A notable feature at one meeting was the number of professionally produced placards bearing the message: 'LOCK UP YOUR GRANNIES. DR DEATH IS HERE.' This was a variant of the media headline that used to appear when the Rolling Stones were in town—'Lock Up Your Daughters'.

As to be expected in a Catholic country such as Ireland, moral outrage in this part of the world is well organised and systemic. Through groups such as the Youth Defence and the Christian Solidarity Party, not to mention the Catholic and Anglican churches, opposition to voluntary euthanasia is everywhere in the Emerald Isle. This has led to the usual cancellation of venues for our events. In fact Dublin still holds the record, with four venues in a row cancelling over the course of two days. Included in this list was the famous Buswells Hotel, which had initially approached us when they heard of our problems. They told me there wouldn't be any issue with us. They'd hosted pro-abortion gatherings with Mary Robinson, political meetings with Sinn Fein, even at the height of the Irish unrest, and never cancelled. Twelve hours later they cancelled, with just a brief phone message; no explanation, no appeal. The problem was solved eventually with the assistance of local groups such as Atheist Ireland.

In Dublin we also saw the infiltration and disruption of our meetings by protestors (something that has rarely happened before). Andrea Williams, CEO of an organisation called Christian Concern, trotted out an argument that was new to me. She said, 'In the context of such a dismal economic climate [in Ireland], Dr Nitschke's message is a great danger to vulnerable people who may feel pressured into taking their own lives'.[3] A line difficult to take seriously.

But there has been an upside. Voluntary euthanasia in Ireland is now an issue that is increasingly discussed and a topic of public debate. While the authorities continue to wield a heavy hand—in 2011 the friend of a terminally ill Exit member was threatened with charges should she accompany her friend to Zurich for an assisted suicide—there is an emergent right-to-die movement in that country. Our meetings, and the media that our visits have attracted, have changed the climate. That Exit now has an Irish chapter, or branch, led by activist Tom Curran, is testimony to this. In 2012 I took part in a debate on the euthanasia issue at the Dublin debating society 'The Phil' at Trinity College, with Tom and Sir Terry Pratchett, and in late 2012 Tom launched his own court action in Ireland, aimed at restoring the right of his long-term partner, Marie, who is severely disabled by multiple sclerosis, to choose when she might die.[4] This important case found its way to the Irish Supreme Court, but in March 2013 her case was dismissed.

Exit's workshop program sees me visit the UK and North America on a regular basis, and I've also often found myself travelling abroad for debates, conferences, talks at medical schools and even literary festivals. I am always keen to extend the Exit meeting-and-workshop program to new countries, but that does require some local support to get things set up. As we offer people better practical end-of-life options, and associated technologies like drug testing, the need to spread the program increases. In 2013 Exit held its first ever workshops in Germany and the Netherlands, and there are now active negotiations to stage such events in South Africa, Israel and Singapore.

In 2009 I was excited to be part of a new cable network channel broadcasting into China. Led by Hong Kong entrepreneur Robert Chua, the thirteen-part series *Dignified Departures* aimed at getting the Chinese middle classes to talk about how to plan ahead for death. I travelled to Hong Kong to participate in the venture and had the chance to learn of some of the subtle cultural differences that exist. This was the first time Chinese mass media had tackled the issue on the mainland, an important milestone.

It never ceases to amaze me that the elderly workshop attendees and conference audiences in places as diverse as India, New Caledonia and even Switzerland all ask much the same question—where do I get my Nembutal, how do I store it for the next twenty years and what will my death be like should I ever drink it? The same applies to journalists, regardless of whether they are from prominent Polish newspapers, such as the *Gazeta Wyborcza*, or the ones asking me questions at the Hong Kong Foreign Correspondents' Club, or tiny regional publications like *Barrier Daily Truth* in Broken Hill. Why do you do it? How many of your patients have you helped/killed? Have you ever been arrested? While emphasis may change from country to country, the strong interest in how we are to die is universal.

SEVENTEEN

Time out

*… George Fraser soldered a broken exhaust pipe for
the headstrong schoolmaster, and begged him not to go
on with the mad project of crossing the desert to Ayer's
Rock in the midsummer heat.*

Frank Clune, *The Red Heart: Sagas of Centralia*,
1940

At times my life has been seriously out of balance. Being
absorbed in various causes—Aboriginal land rights,
resistance to US bases, voluntary euthanasia—that take up
energy and time can seriously effect personal relationships.
Thankfully, that is not the case now. With a partner as involved
in the voluntary euthanasia issue as I am, work and personal
matters are often intertwined, but it is still possible on occasions to step back and enjoy life together—simple things like
camping, the silence of the Outback, a shared enthusiasm for
craft beers, overseas travel, good food, friends and so on. As I
said in an interview a few years back, 'We don't just sit around
talking about death and dying all the time.'

I'm fond of films and music. The quirky *Harold and
Maude*, the first time I'd ever heard of the right age for an
elective death, long before I met Lisette Nigot, and the
ugly *Wake in Fright*, which so captures the atmosphere of
Broken Hill and dispels the romantic outback myth, are

among my favourites. In recent years I've discovered internet radio, which has made my treasured library of old 78s all but obsolete. Going bush, I liked the idea of copying Karen Blixen, with the wind-up gramophone on the fold-up camp table and a slow waltz around the camp site. Now when Fiona and I are out, as long as we are close enough to an Aboriginal community with good internet connectivity, we just tune the iPad to one of the amazing 1930s or 1940s music internet radio stations and bring the sounds of the interwar years into our happy-hour drinks.

Over the years, the way we take time out from work has varied a lot. There's been the occasional trip to Singapore (closer, and cheaper, than Sydney for a short break), the odd five-star hotel in Europe (as a treat), and more than one beer-and-brewery tour in either New Zealand or the US. One motif of home-based holidays is touring on either our motorbike or in the MG through the desert or hills.

My father had motorbikes when I was very young, and my brother Dennis rode one for years and I've always been interested in them. In 1976 or thereabouts, I was walking along Todd Street in Alice Springs when I saw a dishevelled rider covered in oil and dirt pull his motorbike up to the kerb and almost fall into a heap in the gutter. I had a motorbike at the time, a 1955 British Matchless 500cc single cylinder 'thumper', so I knew a bit about classic bikes. I recognised this as one of the relatively new Russian Cossack 650cc, which I commented on.

'Yeah,' he said, 'and if you want it, you can have it.'

He'd come up from Adelaide. In those days, the Stuart Highway was unsealed and known for its corrugations. They were bad and unavoidable, from grader ridge to grader ridge. This poor guy was covered in dust and was still shaking from what had clearly been a very rough ride.

'How much?' I said.

'Four hundred bucks.'

I guessed the bike was about two or three years old. Four hundred dollars wasn't a sensational bargain because the bikes sold new for $650; people used to joke that they cost a dollar a cc. But getting a bike like that in Alice in any other circumstances would have been difficult, and here was one on a plate. I bought it there and then. Later, I bought another one and I kept the original on the road by cannibalising parts from the second.

The Cossack is a Russian copy of a pre–World War II German BMW designed to be fitted with a sidecar—the sort of thing you commonly see in war movies, with a machine-gun mounted on the front, the officer in the sidecar in his leather coat with another stormtrooper doing the hard riding. The Cossack had only a six-volt electrical system, which caused trouble, and brakes so poor that it seemed they'd been added as a late optional extra. The biggest problem though was kick starting, especially with the sidecar fitted; in the Russian Steppes, with a sidecar on the right, a kick starter on the left may have been manageable. But here, forced to mount the chair on the opposite side, kick starting this beast was almost impossible.

The Russians seem to have a knack of making things that might work well, but look as though they're forty years out of date and that was the case with the Cossack. It wasn't pre-war, but looked it. And I racked up a lot of kilometres on it, commuting from Darwin to Sydney for my medical course, across the Plenty Highway, and coming down through Queensland and South Australia, and along the Birdsville on a number of occasions. It performed much better on the open road than in town, and it worked best with the sidecar, especially when I had a genuine Russian one imported and fitted for me by a dodgy neo-Nazi bike shop that used to be on Parramatta Road, just out past Leichhardt.

I decided to attend the fortieth anniversary of the 1966 walk-off from Wave Hill Station in August 2006. ABC TV's

Aboriginal current affairs program, *Message Stick*, had contacted me to say they were making a documentary called 'Ripples from Wave Hill'.[1] They knew of my involvement and wanted some film of me going back for the reunion. I liked that idea and thought I'd take my old Toyota, which had first taken me out there in 1973 and had become well known during my time there. I had kept it registered over all the years, and had run it intermittently, but it needed a lot of work. When I pulled the engine down I found the head was badly cracked; it couldn't be welded and I couldn't get a replacement in time. So we decided to travel by motorbike to the reunion.

The ABC filmed me on the motorbike as a sort of mock-up of my original journey to Wave Hill, although, of course, it hadn't been anything like that. Fiona and I went down with our camping gear strapped on at the back of the sidecar. The weekend was structured with various activities, including a procession and a re-enactment of the walk-off. There were a lot of emotional moments. Kev Carmody was there and he sang 'From Little Things Big Things Grow', and I was able to talk with Hoppy Mick Rangiari. It was the last time I saw Hoppy Mick, who died not long after. He was the last of the active members of the strike. I recognised a few people around who were just kids when I was first there decades earlier.

Gabi Hollows, Fred's widow, and Peter Garrett attended, each surrounded by a large entourage. David Quinn, who I barely recognised, was also there. It was the first time I'd seen him since our fight at Top Springs Pub some thirty-five years earlier. We talked briefly, without hostility. I also met Tom Uren, a minister in the Whitlam government. I'd admired him for a long time and he had been a friend and boxing opponent of my old boss in Parks and Wildlife, Bob Darken. He said some nice things about my work

There were very strict rules about camping at the site, so I did as I always had and rode a few kilometres down the track to camp off in the bush. It felt good to go back. I couldn't get to the forty-fifth anniversary in 2011, and had to watch it on television. I'm determined to be there for the fiftieth.

★ ★ ★

In 2006 Fiona and I took a long overdue holiday together. We planned a motorbike trip from Sydney to the Territory. But there is a preamble to this story.

During my medical studies in the 1980s I would travel back to Alice Springs at every opportunity. It was on one of these visits that I was browsing some old books of my father's, including one called *The Red Heart* by Frank Clune. It was a collection of short non-fiction stories and one story was about Ellis Bankin, a schoolteacher from Glenroy, in Melbourne, who rode his 350cc Triumph motorbike to all kinds of places across Australia in his school holidays in the 1930s. During the summer holidays in 1936, he attempted to become the first to ever ride by motorbike to Uluru, but he didn't make it. Instead, Bankin lost his way, ran out of fuel and died of dehydration under a mulga tree near Mount Conner, about a hundred kilometres east of the Rock. The motorbike was found intact when a search party finally located his body, and he was buried where he lay. The owner of the old Lynda Vale station, only 16 kilometres from where Ellis died, put up a headstone and erected a post-and-rail fence around the grave.

I was intrigued by this story. This was in 1985, and I realised that the fiftieth anniversary of Ellis's death was approaching. I wanted to find out more and started by ringing all people with the name Bankin who lived in Victoria. Quite quickly I located Frank, Ellis Bankin's brother, who was then living in the Dandenongs, to Melbourne's east. He said I was the second person who had recently inquired about Ellis. The other person had been Dick Duckworth, a motorcycle enthusiast and amateur historian, who lived in Yarraville.

I met up with Dick and the idea of marking the fiftieth anniversary of Ellis Bankin's tragic journey was formed. We both thought the grave might become a significant destination for adventurous motorcyclists to visit.

The grave is on the Curtin Springs station and, as it happened, I knew Peter Severin, the station owner, from my time as a ranger, and made contact. I'd arranged for some pre-publicity in an article published in *Motorcycle News* magazine and on a hot January evening in 1986, on the anniversary of Bankin's death, Dick and I and a dozen or so people—some local pastoralists, some motor-cycle enthusiasts from Alice Springs—held a small ceremony at pretty much the exact time Bankin was thought to have died.[2] The headstone and the post-and-rail fence were still there, although the worse for wear after fifty years. I had a brass plaque made up in Sydney to commemorate the anniversary, and we bolted this onto one of the posts to mark the event. Dave Richardson, a journalist from the *Centralian Advocate*, also came and recorded the event in a double-page spread in his paper. I was pleased that this indomitable character, who wasn't as widely known as he deserved to be, finally had some recognition. Dick Duckworth self-published a book on Bankin in 1977, called *Ellis Matthewman Bankin: Outback Motorcyclist Who Perished: A Biography*, and it includes a photograph of my motorbike sitting there on a sand dune.

The year 2006 would be the seventieth anniversary of Bankin's death and I thought, *Why not make it our holiday to go to the gravesite by motorbike?* Fiona liked the idea. I had the bike trucked from Darwin to Sydney and we left from Kings Cross, going up over the Blue Mountains to Bathurst, west to Broken Hill and Yunta. The plan was to go through the north Flinders Ranges, up to Oodnadatta and on to Finke, then to turn off towards Mount Conner and the gravesite. We would then finish the holiday heading up to Alice and on to Darwin, camping all the way. We were carrying food, water and plenty of extra fuel.

All went well until, while we were camping north of Oodnadatta on the Finke road, Fiona discovered she'd lost her bag and some precious photographs. There was no option. The next day we rode back to Oodnadatta and spoke to the police. There had been a crowd of locals looking at the bike when we were refuelling and we thought the bag must have been stolen. Just as the interrogation of the locals was about to start, a truck driver radioed through to the Pink Roadhouse saying that he'd seen the bag lying by the side of the road and that it could now be collected up the track at Hamilton Station. We were to pay for this delay. As we left Oodnadatta, reports were coming in of heavy rain in the area, and we were advised to get back to the bitumen before the storm stuck. We did make the main Oodnadatta–Marla road, which was better, but still not sealed. That night the storm hit; first the swirling dust and sand, then sheet after sheet of rain until everything was flooded. We would spend the next two days struggling to get the bike unbogged from one spot, only to see the wheels sink down a few metres further along the road. I had to deflate the tyres to get some traction, and then pump them up again with a hand pump, only to make about 50 metres before again sinking into the mud. This was done over and over, until we were both exhausted and it was clear that we couldn't go on; we would just have to wait the weather out. There was no traffic and we knew the road had been closed. Our sleeping gear and everything else was drenched, every-thing except a precious box of matches. We'd also run out of coffee and beer, but surrounded by water and with plenty of flour, it was clear we'd survive.

The following morning, a light plane flew over and Fiona started marking out a giant 'HELP' sign on the road, and running round trying to use her reflective helmet visor to attract the pilot's attention. I thought this was a little over the top. We weren't in any real danger. Uncomfortable yes, but we could have safely sat there for a fortnight. Hard, I thought, explaining a giant 'HELP' sign on the road. In any event, the plane flew on, and we sat for another day and another night. On day three, a four-wheel drive appeared in the distance and slowly crawled its way through the mud to our campsite.

The driver of the Toyota was Doug Lillecrapp of Todmorden Station and pilot of the light plane that had previously flown over. He had driven out from the station to see what damage the rain had caused, and offered to help us get back to the bitumen at Marla. Our gear was moved from the bike to his truck, and Fiona rode in the front seat. The sun had emerged and the road was starting to dry out, and with an unloaded bike and an empty sidecar, we finally made it to Marla. From there, we had to abandon any hopes of getting to the Bankin grave; we had simply run out of time. Instead, we travelled south to Coober Pedy. Fiona booked into a motel, and I flew out to Perth for two days to launch the election campaign for Steve Walker, an independent standing in the coming West Australian state election.

That was the end of the Outback trek. It was certainly a break from work and it provided us with some great moments. We still laugh about the fact that even though the Exit staff all noticed we were missing, none of them thought there was any point in contacting the police. We may just have needed that giant 'HELP' sign after all.

EIGHTEEN

Day by day

We don't sit around talking about death and dying all the time.

Philip Nitschke, 2008

My days are busy, damn busy, and have been for years. But it was entrepreneur Dick Smith, at the Festival of Dangerous Ideas in Sydney, who made me take a step back. After our joint panel presentation, Dick asked me casually, 'How do you make your living?' My standard response to this question goes something like, 'Oh, people who like what I do make donations; it's hand-to-mouth, but we get by.'

This is an automatic response developed over many years, the aim of which is to keep the conversation short. But, in truth, making a living as a voluntary euthanasia activist is a hell of a lot harder than this makes it sound. The task is two-fold. First, voluntary euthanasia must be kept on the public agenda; the principal way of doing this is via the media. Second, I have to pay the bills. When I gave up a full-time medical practice in the late 1990s I took a considerable pay cut. This didn't matter—I've never been driven by the dollar. But, these days, I have an organisation that needs funds to undertake its activities and I have a small staff who need to be paid. My waking hours are spent managing these two driving factors. I need constantly to devise new ways of encouraging the public to show their support by becoming members of Exit International, or by paying to come to a workshop, which is the fee-for-service side. Donations are a bonus that help keep Exit afloat financially and allow me to continue.

These financial needs of running an organisation are balanced every day against our political aims of promoting a law reform agenda and ensuring those who seek end-of-life options are well serviced. Most of the time, these two goals are compatible. For example, exposure in the media not only brings new members (and sells more books) but it ensures that voluntary euthanasia remains in the public's eye, and may even prompt a politician or two to change their position.

As I explained earlier, working with the media is relentless, delicate and time consuming. Not only do we need Exit members, or other members of the public, to tell their stories and share their lives, often at a time of incredible stress and anxiety, but this also needs to fit in the media's interest in covering the issue. It does occasionally happen, when the needs of Exit and the media coincide, but it is a bit like the alignment of the planets. It's naïve to expect a newspaper to run a story on voluntary euthanasia every week and they're the first to remind you that they are not your gun for hire. The media will only cover a story on some aspect of voluntary euthanasia or interview a suffering person seeking help when it suits them, and there's usually nothing I can do to make them change their minds. Commonly, though, I spend my days talking to, cajoling and sometimes even fighting off journalists. Like them, I often feel as though I am only as good as my next story.

And then there are the subjects. Most people who are dying want their privacy, and don't want what's left of their lives talked about and publicised. Even if the family are committed voluntary euthanasia supporters and don't want the death of their loved one to be in vain, they don't necessarily want to be dragged into the spotlight. It is a very special person and a special family who will trust their cape and take the leap. This can be extremely frustrating, as I see opportunities for social and legislative change pass by, all because this or that person won't talk to the media. While I try to be sympathetic, I am also often very frustrated that a refusal to speak often means that the big picture remains unchallenged and unchanged. When a person gets their Nembutal and has their options settled they are often overjoyed, and keen to withdraw from the issue, but this doesn't help others. In the long run, change is needed. Every day I see people quietly using their drugs and leaving the planet. It is good that they have that choice, but I just wish they'd spoken out before they went; the activist in me can be hard-hearted at times.

Working with and trying to use the media this way may sound like prostitution and, yes, I have been accused more than once of being a media slut. But, as Fairfax journalist Gay Alcorn once pointed out, my living and my organisation now depend on it; no longer can I rely on the sheltered medical workshop available to all Australian doctors. If voluntary euthanasia fades from the national agenda, there will be even less hope of change. And, if people don't support my work, Exit's bills will not get paid. Unlike others in the non-profit sector, we have no government grants to fall back on. Each dollar that comes our way is as much a product of strategic planning and hard work as it is a vote of confidence in who we are and what we stand for.

Taking a step back from media, we are always looking for an innovative strategy to highlight the issue. One recent opportunity that presented itself was the chance to run a test case on voluntary euthanasia, in particular looking at the argument that the seriously ill are discriminated against by current law, because they have lost the ability to suicide. It is a rights issue, and we have been in talks with a leading law firm that is interested in running a test case on this issue. While they are offering their services pro bono, finding the right person and family to base it on, and then finding the exact legal hook to hang the whole project on, is a major challenge. If this gets off the ground, it will be the product of a huge amount of background work, but a positive declaration on a legal question such as this would have immense value and could well precipitate action.

On a week-to-week basis, my time is divided between being on the road and holding workshops and public meetings in Australia, Europe, North America and New Zealand, or the respite times between. When I'm not travelling, I start the day with jogging, which I find is as good for my head as for my heart. This is a daily indulgence that I try never to sacrifice. Once back home and in the office, however, the best-planned day can develop a mind of its own as I troubleshoot from one thing to the next. On bad days, I find myself running in circles and having very little to show for it. On other days, visible leaps forward are made. The trick to survival is an ability to multi-task and to manage time. And, since our small core of five staff all work from home across three countries, it can be challenging. My long-time business manager in Queensland has long since learned to read my mind.

Quite often, Exit will have a number of important issues or projects on the go at any one time—we have to—and we must carefully ration the projects we embrace, prioritising them depending on their importance, cost and time needed to develop them. The limiting factor is usually money. When Exit's fortunes improve, with a bequest for example, the number of projects we undertake increases. Any one week could involve the scheduling of, and doing the mailing out for, workshops in the US, dealing with programs such as *60 Minutes* in Australia, ensuring the next shipment of Max Dog nitrogen is on its way to those who have ordered it, talking to and counselling terminally ill patients who call in and who would like a face-to-face visit, speaking at public debates and conferences (events that are as often overseas), preparing and publishing updates to our online *Peaceful Pill eHandbook*, which is still produced in the US and, related to this, updating the online Peaceful Pill forums (which have more than three thousand active members worldwide), staying up until the early morning to join an Exit webinar in the UK, or research and experimental work in my laboratory and learning how to use Exit's newest piece of laboratory equipment. Time for reflection fits somewhere in between and there are rarely enough hours in the day. I can't describe how much I look forward to my quiet beer and the chance to relax each night.

But would I change this life? Not likely. Like others who are self-employed, I treasure being my own boss, deciding what issues to pursue, and having a work life that is so varied. While I have a board of directors at Exit, the day-to-day running of it is at my discretion. Of course the down side of this is that when our Exit members are unhappy, or feel that their needs have been ignored or overlooked, then the responsibility is mine, and with no one else to blame, I have to take their criticisms on board; it is a foolish person who does not listen to the complaints and advice of others. But, no, despite the frantic rate at which I often have to travel, I would not change this life.

NINETEEN

Looking ahead

The future belongs to those who prepare for it today.

Malcom X

I'm occasionally asked what I've done about succession planning at Exit. As things stand, I realise, I can't exactly delegate my central function. This is something I have agonised over, as the issue comes up from time to time with Exit members. I realise many groups share this conundrum but I guess not all are as highly individualised as Exit has become. I've asked Fiona, and she said she would think about it. A medical background might help, but it's certainly not essential. Initially I thought a young doctor who was looking for a challenging life project—rather than settling down into the security of a regular medical practice—might come forward, but as yet, no one has. And who can blame them? This can be thankless work. I have stayed at it, not only because it is something I believe in deeply, but because I've been able to successfully blend my personal and work life. I'm not sure how many others would find themselves in this lucky position.

I don't plan to leave the organisation any time soon, and, like many of my generation, I like to think I'm going to live forever. I'm a believer in the benefits of aerobic exercise and fitness, although this may stem more from my hypochondria than a search for longevity. My daily exercise routine is something I quite literally could not live without.

My father had a heart attack at sixty-five, then lived another ten years with his damaged health before succumbing to progressive heart failure. I don't want that. When I was a postgraduate student at Flinders University, and interested in exercise, I came across the Harvard step test and liked the idea of being able to quantify things like fitness. The step test was devised as a cheap and easy way to screen young men entering the military in World War II. It involves stepping up and back down 50 centimetres 150 times in five minutes, followed by a five-minute recovery phase with sequential heart rate readings and use of the formula. A count of 100 shows an excellent level of cardiac fitness. It's not an easy exercise; at university I persuaded every one I could to try the test, smugly looking on as many failed to complete it. I've done it intermittently for the past fifty years and, these days watch with some concern as the index slowly declines.

Another reason for not being too concerned about an Exit succession plan relates to my changing attitude to the voluntary euthanasia issue and likely developments. When I first became involved, I thought that the Northern Territory legislation would start an inevitable process that would put an end to the bigoted and inhumane attitudes that opposed a person's right to a peaceful death. The Kevin Andrews Act scotched those hopes. Over time, I've parted company, ideologically, with those who still see changes in legislation as the single ultimate goal.

Legislation is, by its nature, limiting, and most models that now exist only address the needs of those who are extremely (usually terminally) ill. As I often quip when referring back to the Northern Territory model, you just about had to be dead to qualify! It was as though the state was saying, 'Okay, you've only got a short time left, so, we've decided to let you go.' While some newer models, such as the New Zealand End of Life Choices Bill, proposed by MP Maryan Street, does recognise chronic suffering rather than terminal illness, and does have provision for written advance directives if a person should lose the ability to communicate, even this most progressive model is still anchored in the concept of the state granting authority, rather that the patient (or even a well person) having this choice as a basic right. There is a growing number of people who want the choice of controlling the timing and manner of their death not only because they are terminally ill, but for all kinds of other (often non-medical) reasons. A quadriplegic who has had enough, the long-term partner who doesn't want to live on after the death of their loved one, the ninety year old (like my mother) who sees little point in living on after all her friends have gone. These people will never have their need served by the passage of voluntary euthanasia legislation. To my mind, their best hope is with the development of better and more accessible means of peacefully ending life. Exit International increasingly reflects this view.

When asked to look ahead, say, ten years, I'm not particularly optimistic about possible law reform, even though there is a certain inevitability about it. In Australia, Tasmania and South Australia remain the states 'most likely' to legalise some form of voluntary euthanasia. However, the current swing to the right in most states, along with in the Federal Parliament, doesn't augur well. In many ways, the issue is much hotter in the US, where the Citizen Initiated Referendum (ballot) process allows the public at the state level to pass laws with the same force and effect as parliamentary legislation.[1] In the UK, too, the government has been forced to confront the legislative environment, given the sheer number of locals crossing the Chanel to make use of the Dignitas service in Zurich.

In the UK in 2010, the Department of Public Prosecutions, prompted by the Debbie Purdy case, relaxed the guidelines on who is and is not likely to be prosecuted due to assisting a suicide.[2] While hardly an instance of law reform, it is an important first step. Others are using the UK's courts to mount legal challenges. Another important recent case, one in which I was involved as an expert witness, made use of the defence of 'necessity' to the crime of murder. Following a stroke in 2005, Tony Nicklinson developed 'locked in' syndrome.[3] This meant that while his body had no movement, his mind was unaffected. Tony could blink, but little else, and communication was a nightmare. He wanted to die; the problem was how. Even in Switzerland, you need to be able to drink the Nembutal yourself. Tony's legal case revolved around his effective discrimination as a disabled person; his 'illness' was denying him his right to suicide.

My involvement with Tony concerned modifications to the Deliverance Machine. With Ted Huber, a friend from Flinders University days, I worked on a wireless interface that would allow Tony to self-administer his own lethal drugs. Of course, Tony's family GP would have needed to prescribe the drugs. Jane and Tony's two adult daughters, Lauren and Beth, would have loaded the drugs into the machine and connected it to his stomach peg but, literally with the blink of an eye, Tony could have had the peaceful death he wanted. I became involved when Tony's QC, Paul Bowen, made contact to see if I would be interested in joining the team. Under current UK law, a murder charge was a distinct possibility if anyone were to help him get his wish. A High Court case was an attempt to ensure that Tony got his peaceful death, without any legal carnage left behind. Sadly, after losing the initial court hearing, Tony died of pneumonia a short time later.[4] A case like this takes me full circle and once again stresses to the potential of technology and its important role in the ongoing euthanasia debate. Technology that can get around legal hurdles, technology that makes things possible, makes things happen.

On this note, in recent years my work has changed direction. While I am still committed to holding workshops, the debate has moved well beyond 'Voluntary Euthanasia 101'. With our members' increased level of know-how, new challenges are emerging and our the elderly supporters are actively racing ahead, getting their practical options sorted.

Several years ago, I happened upon China as a source of laboratory-grade sodium pentobarbital. According to *The New York Times*, chemical companies in China, unlike drug companies, go largely unregulated, and we'd discovered a source of powdered Nembutal that is relatively easy to access.

Once this information was verified, we published the news in *The Peaceful Pill eHandbook*. While we were not encouraging our readers to import the drug, we noted that it was now readily available. Not unexpectedly, many took the plunge and broke the law, often for the first time in their lives. They did this to ensure that they had choice and independence, safely stored, a comfort to them as they aged.

The availability of this new form of the drug, however, has brought problems of its own. I'm constantly asked, 'How do I know that this packet of white powder that arrived in the mail is the real stuff?' 'How do I know if it's pure?' 'How do I know it will "do the job" if I ever take it?' These are questions that only science and technology can solve.

To take choice to the next level, I have embarked on a mobile drug-testing service, and the development of a quantitative home test kit to enable people to test the purity of the drug. Exit now offers the equipment required so that elderly members who have imported powder they believe to be Nembutal can come to the laboratory and do their own purity testing, and a home kit for a quick, but less accurate, measurement in the privacy of their home. The appeal of a long shelf life is clear. Get the drug, test it, store it correctly and get on with living; sort out this issue once and for all and put your own safety net in place. In the broadest terms, this is the future I see, rather than an ongoing battle for legislative reform, and it is for this reason that succession planning at Exit is not that important to me. My critics though, are quick to ask, exactly who should be able to get this precious powder? The depressed teens of the world? Of course not, although, over time, my position has broadened.

I now believe the ideal situation would be for Nembutal to be available to every adult of sound mind over the age of fifty who seeks it. Naturally, there would be grey areas—for example, the definition of a sound mind, and what about the cut off age? But these things could be worked through. Like all big ethical issues, voluntary euthanasia raises some complicated questions that, while not unanswerable, deserve serious consideration. A concern I have long had is in regard to prisoners who have life sentences, as for some people, life in prison is a form of torture. Although I'm totally opposed to capital punishment, the question is, should prisoners with no prospect of ever being released be given the option of voluntary euthanasia? I think the answer is clear: if the state is going to engage in this form of torture, it should at least be prepared to offer those incarcerated a peaceful death. Anything less is barbaric.

In 2009, I was approached by the Public Defenders Office in Cleveland, Ohio, to help challenge the legal decision to execute murderer Kenneth Biros. In November of that year, Ohio became the first state to adopt the one-drug protocol for lethal injections. The usual practice had been to administer the barbiturate thiopentone, which leads to loss of consciousness, and then to follow up with a curare-like drug and finally potassium to stop the condemned prisoner's heart. The proposed 'single drug protocol' was an attempt to avoid the grim consequence of administering too much of the paralysing drug curare, after insufficient thiopentone. Another concern was that thiopentone, or Pentothal as it is commonly known, was becoming very difficult to source and attention turned to possibly using a single intravenous administration of sodium pentobarbital, or Nembutal. As one of the few people to have ever had experience of intravenously using this drug to end life, the question I was asked was whether there was any argument I could think of that would preclude its use in executions. I worked with the office over a period of months, but it was difficult to see how we could mount a case against the use of Nembutal in executions, while supporting its use as the best voluntary euthanasia agent. Ken Biros died by lethal injection on 8 December that year. His death may have been efficient, although hardly the type of elective peaceful end that Exit seeks. His death, as with all deaths from capital punishment, was an obscenity.

I'm sometimes asked about my own death. Well, I face the same dilemmas as everyone else. I dread the thought of leaving behind those I love. I also don't want to die in some hospital, clouded with drugs, tethered to tubes and monitors. If I'm lucky enough, it'll be a bottle of Nembutal in the Gibson Desert, leaving what's left of my body to the western crows. I've spoken about this with Fiona, who has promised to help make it happen, if needs be.

And I'm occasionally asked, 'What about a political career?' Well, what about it? While there is a handful of politicians I admire, parliament is probably not the best place for me. I would have trouble functioning in an institution that sees every issue of importance as a two-sided battle between warring factions. I'd also have trouble finding any political party that would want me as a member, or one in which I'd want to be a member, although I have recently become an enthusiastic supporter of the newly formed Voluntary Euthanasia Party, initiated by Corey McCann. As I've realised through my several election campaigns standing as an independent in the seat of Menzies and elsewhere, this can be a hard road, and getting any message out during an election is difficult. But with a party behind you, and in particular the Voluntary Euthanasia Party, well, maybe that's got possibilities. Personally, though, I think it may be better for me to be working as an activist in the community, if not on voluntary euthanasia, then on other issues that concern me, such the size of the world's population, the exploitation of natural resources and the associated deterioration of the planet and damage to our precious plant and animal life.

And it's just as well I have other interests and concerns. At the time of writing, there is a major threat looming for my work as a doctor and as voluntary euthanasia activist, in that that AHPRA is once again trying to take away my medical registration. At the end of 2012 there were two concurrent investigations into my fitness to practise medicine. The first inquiry stemmed from my idea of using the Therapeutic Goods Administration's Special Access Scheme (SAS) to possibly lawfully import Nembutal to be used as a sleep agent.

'Wendy' was a terminally ill woman from Victor Harbor in South Australia, who made contact with Exit on 31 May 2011. Two weeks earlier, she had been diagnosed with Motor Neurone Disease (MND). Determined not to end up paralysed and at risk of choking on her own saliva, Wendy joined Exit, bought *The Peaceful Pill eHandbook* and requested a clinic visit with me. A few months earlier, in March 2011, Australian Customs issued an information sheet titled *Importing Barbiturates: Pentobarbital/Nembutal* that stressed the illegality of such importation, except in the very special circumstances covered under the Special Access Scheme of Australia's Therapeutic Goods Administration (TGA). 'Special access' enables medical professionals to apply for the lawful importation into Australia of unapproved drugs for prescription to terminally ill people. The Customs article gave me an idea. Instead of breaking the law by illegally importing the drug, Wendy and a number of other terminally ill patients I had could apply to make use of the SAS. Wendy certainly fulfilled the necessary criteria of being a 'Category A' patient. Under Australia's Medical Device Regulations, Category A is defined as 'persons who are seriously ill with a condition from which death is reasonably likely to occur within a matter of months ...'

At the time, Wendy had been unable to get a satisfactory night's sleep and had been unsuccessfully self-medicating, using her partner's valium. Subsequent prescriptions of other sleeping medications, including Phenobarbital, had all failed her. This is perhaps not surprising, as MND is notorious for interrupting its sufferers' sleep. While I planned to warn Wendy not to misuse the drug, ultimately that would have been up to her, as it is with any drug a doctor prescribes. However, things never got that far. As soon as I submitted the initial application (stage 1) of the approval process, AHPRA received a formal complaint from the TGA. The TGA based its complaint on media reports suggesting that the application was made solely to facilitate the patient's suicide, and accused me of acting contrary to 'good medical practice'.

At this point, Wendy knew that the special access scheme of the TGA would not be possible for her. Like so many in her situation, she didn't have time on her side. As she wrote in her suicide note:

> Motor Neurone Disease is an awful disease. It deprives a person of their dignity and independence. It also provides an awful death when swallowing becomes impossible and one is trapped in a paralysis which has no end.
>
> My decision to end my suffering rather than waiting for the disease to finally take hold of me is a long and considered one.
>
> To this end I have spent the past few months acquiring the drugs that I would need.

On 11 December 2011, Wendy drank the Nembutal she had obtained illegally via the internet. She was sixty-one years old.

The TGA complaint started a long process of investigation by AHPRA into my 'fitness to practise medicine'. Years later, I still have no idea what the outcome of this lengthy enquiry will be.

More insidious was the second investigation launched in August 2012, again to establish whether I was 'fit and proper' enough to hold medical registration. The second enquiry started while the first was still running. That AHPRA was to initiate a new investigation was made known to *The Australian* newspaper long before I was even informed. When I complained to the regulator about this issue, they denied any complicity, claiming I should have ensured my mailing address was up to date. I still left wondering then how *The Australian*'s Dennis Shanahan could bill his article as an 'exclusive'?[5]

The issue this time concerned my involvement in the distribution of Max Dog nitrogen cylinders. In recent years, my research focus into the use of gases to provide a peaceful death has shifted from the use of helium to the use of nitrogen gas. In terms of efficacy, any inert gas will work with an Exit bag; a significant and unique advantage of nitrogen though is that it cannot be detected at autopsy. For many elderly Exit members, what is ultimately written on one's death certificate *is* important. They say they don't want to be known in the family in years to come as 'old Aunt Mabel who suicided', especially if they were to take this step after some long battle with cancer. Nitrogen also has the added benefit that the Max Dog cylinders are refillable, the gauges are more precise and, if any leakage does occur over the years while the cylinder is in storage, the gas can simply be topped up.

In his many-paged complaint to AHPRA, right-to-life activist Paul Russell claimed that Max Dog was a product used purely for suicide. He was wrong, and I trust the investigators at AHPRA will realise this. A visit to one of the many beer festivals running around the world will show the growing interest in the home use of nitrogen for dispensing craft beer. (While Guinness has long been partially gassed by nitrogen, rather than carbon dioxide, it is a much more recent development for other beer to be served this way. The effect is a beer that is creamy and, some say, more fulsome in flavour.) Exit organised Australia's first 'Nitro Night' at the Wheatsheaf Hotel ('The Wheaty') in Adelaide in March 2013. Max Dog sponsored the evening and gave those attending the opportunity to compare the difference when beer is served using nitrogen rather than the traditional carbon dioxide.

Of course, for a death by hypoxia to look unsuspicious, the equipment will all need to be removed. This presents another dilemma, in that most Crimes Acts contain an offence called 'misconduct with regard to corpses', or some similar phrasing, although the penalty for such an offence is generally pretty lenient; nothing like the years in jail that could result from actively assisting.

What surprised me most about the second AHPRA investigation was the blatant political nature of the complaint. Russell openly acknowledged that he 'would like to see Nitschke's work and Exit International shut down'. While I am, of course, answerable to the law, Russell's complaint to AHPRA was not legal in character; nor was it medical. And that is the point. In my response to AHPRA, I stated:

> I do not understand there to be any suggestion that I am lacking in appropriate knowledge or skills, nor in concern or commitment to the health of patients or people in general. I do not understand there to be any suggestion that I have been negligent in the treatment of patients, nor failed to observe any relevant standard of performance in medical practice.

As *Australian* columnist Ross Fitzgerald wrote, 'Nitschke says he feels this is a quasi-religious, political witch-hunt'.[6] How right he is. What is AHPRA doing meddling in church politics such as this?

Once again, lawyers are working pro bono in defending me. Indeed, offers of assistance have come from a number of surprising quarters, including some from the medical and legal professions, and also from the media. This support is greatly appreciated as the pressure to push me from the medical profession mounts. In social media quarters, a Facebook campaign to save my registration has been created and Twitter has proved an effective way of keeping supporters up to date with developments. I am damned if I do attempt to help those who are desperate to die, and I'd also be damned if I turned my back and walked away from them. This nebulous 'fit and proper' criteria applied in such a discretionary manner is hard to argue against. To those who believe in God, I will never be 'fit and proper', but should I be a doctor?

If AHPRA makes such a decision when they finally end their long-running investigations, I could not only be suspended from practise but permanently deregistered as a doctor. While I'll do what I can to stay registered, maybe it is just as well that I am prepared to turn my attention to other issues, and even other careers, should the worst come to pass. Chief among my potential new careers is to try life on the stage, doing stand-up comedy. I have already found an agent who sees the potential in this, and I am working on my first script.

My decade and a half of working with those close to death has brought many tears of sadness but also a good deal of joy and laughter. My persecution at the hands of fundamentalists in both medicine and the church is, if nothing else, grist for my comedy mill. It was Ernest Hemingway who said, 'A man's got to take a lot of punishment to write a really funny book.' I hope the same might be said for going on the stage because that, for sure, applies to me. I do now have a head rich in stories of people, places, death and dying. Many tragic, but some hysterically funny, and all of them entertaining. I'd like to think there are worse things than dying laughing.

A note from Peter Corris

As any filmmaker will tell you it can take time to get a project up. Clint Eastwood is said to have taken seven years to bring the Oscar-winning *Unforgiven* to the screen. Some things that seem to be crying out to be done meet unforeseen obstacles.

This book represents my third attempt to collaborate with Philip Nitschke in the writing of his autobiography. Some years ago, after I'd successfully and enjoyably carried out a similar exercise with Fred Hollows, environmentalist John Sinclair and actor Ray Barrett, I was keen to do similar work. Since the publication of those books, I'd been approached several times by people seeking my help. I declined because their stories did not meet the criteria I'd set for myself. I was interested in people who'd had active, not merely cerebral, lives, and, above all, people I admired. My agent contacted Philip to see if he was interested and a meeting was arranged.

We met in one of my favourite places in Sydney—the University Motel in Glebe. Now demolished, it had a seedy history as one of the places where prostitute Sallie-Anne Huckstepp used to take her clients. I'd stayed there myself and frequently used it as 'safe house' or assignation point in my Cliff Hardy novels. It was cheap.

Philip was in one of back rooms, away from the traffic. We sat and talked for about an hour and had a beer. I liked him immediately—finding him direct and unpretentious—but he was very busy. There was talk of a film and other ventures and he reckoned it was premature to think about an autobiography.

I was disappointed but accepted his decision. Euthanasia and Philip Nitschke were frequently in the news and I kept an eye on developments. The next approach came about five years later from Philip himself and his partner, Fiona Stewart. The time seemed right.

We had several meetings—with one publisher at my agent's office, with another at the publisher's city office. I'd read *Killing Me Softly,* the book Philip and Fiona had published in 2005, and some press cuttings they had provided. I prepared a 'pitch' document they approved of for the publishers. But I realised this was not your ordinary autobiography. It would take a particular character to get the project off the ground. That person would be Louise Adler at MUP, who had recently attended a workshop in Melbourne run by Philip. She was impressed, as anyone who has seen him in action as a presenter—diffident but forceful, modest, compelling, anecdotal and funny—would be. Louise is married to Max Gillies, who I'd known at Melbourne High School in the 1950s and had occasional friendly meetings with ever since. Louise contacted me, saying she was keen to publish Philip's autobiography. I was enthusiastic and things went on from there.

I conducted ten interviews with Philip between August 2010 and April 2012. Several of these were in Philip's and Fiona's tiny unit at Kings Cross, several in my place at Newtown and, crucially, one in Darwin in December 2011. Given how significant Darwin and the Northern Territory have been in the Nitschke story, it was important to have some first-hand experience of the place. The Wet wasn't the best time and, in the aftermath of the visit by the President of the United States, the city had a subdued air, but I saw Parliament House, where the ROTI Act was passed, and the hospital where the Nitschke-inspired 'FREE SPEECH?' banner flew for hours in defiance of the authorities.

At the property Philip and Fiona have outside Darwin, I saw the conditions under which he carries out scientific experiments. I also saw the Cossack motorcycle that figures largely in one chapter, and what might be considered the detritus of his adventurous life—the 4WD truck he and Marlies drove from Darwin to Perth, and the decaying boat that replaced the ill-fated *Squizz*. All this helped to provide texture and atmospherics to accompany Philip's account of events.

I saw, too, what Philip had said in his first book, *Killing Me Softly*, about the police invasion that resulted in them breaking into containers, taking away more material than the search warrant permitted and subsequent government embarrassment: 'The police cars swept up the drive …' I'd imagined a concrete strip. In fact, it is a dusty, weed-strewn track.

There were two major difficulties in getting the job done. The first was simply the hectic pace of Philip and Fiona's activities. They were overseas, they were in several different states, they had only two days in Sydney … We fitted in the interviews as best we could, complemented by phone calls and emails.

The second difficulty came when, a week before Christmas, with much of the work done but with still a lot to do, I was hit by a truck, and suffered a smashed elbow and a broken leg, which put me in a rehab hospital for six weeks. For much of that time, I had a cast on my arm and couldn't write and, although I had my own room, there was no way to spread the working drafts, transcripts and other papers around it. Philip visited me after the surgery, a visit that got a mention in the media. All publicity is good publicity.

Things went on hold but there was a slight side benefit. In this book, Philip describes the severe injury to his foot that put him on crutches and into hydrotherapy for a long period. I came to know exactly what that was like.

Philip Nitschke easily met my criteria for a collaborative autobiography—an active life, devoted to a cause I approve of, and pursued with a courage and commitment I admire. It was my task to help bring these qualities into sharp focus.

Notes

1 A good idea

1 Many years later, I found myself speaking opposite Professor
Lickiss at a dinner at the Australian Academy of Forensic
Sciences in Sydney. Her views hadn't changed. As well,
during her contribution, she engaged in word play on
'Nazi—Nitschke—Euthanasia', intimating that my role in
voluntary euthanasia was somehow the same as the Nazis'
role in the Holocaust. I was quietly pleased when the then
Commonwealth Solicitor, General David Bennett, in a
question from the audience, pulled her up for the inappro-
priateness of her innuendo.

2 See: www.abc.net.au/radionational/programs/background
briefing/push-your-vote-our-way/3556506

5 Wave Hill

1 Historical photos can be seen at: www.gurindjifreedomday.
com/bedford%20truck%20stories.html

8 The Top End

1 See: www.abc.net.au/news/2009-05-26/bid-to-keep-
killers-locked-up/1695000

2 See Chris Ryan 'Sex Videos for Research: MP', *Sydney
Morning Herald*, 1 December 1997, p. 2.

9 First in the world

1 See: www.heraldsun.com.au/entertainment/jeremy-sims-
blarney-falls-flat/story-e6frf9o6-1225856123482

2 See: www.youtube.com/watch?v=gdiQScBQDRs

3 See: www.sciencemuseum.org.uk/broughttolife/objects/
display.aspx?id=91717

4 See: www.youtube.com/watch?v=U9O3RjQDtpM

5 See: www.smh.com.au/articles/2002/05/30/1022569809
397.html

10 The overturn

1 Anthony Albanese's speech against the Kevin Andrews Bill can
be viewed at: www.youtube.com/watch?v=x5fs-ZXntxo

2 http://parlinfo.aph.gov.au/parlInfo/search/display/display.
w3p;query=Id%3A%22chamber%2Fhansardr%2F1996-
11-06%2F0170%22 Wednesday, 6 November 1996, page:
6751, Main Committee, EUTHANASIA LAWS BILL
1996, Second Reading.

3 For the transcript of 'The Dying Game', see: www.abc.net.
au/4corners/stories/s72769.htm

11 Moving on

1 See: www.theage.com.au/national/this-is-angelique-she-
wanted-to-die-with-dignity-20080912-4fi2.html; see also
www.youtube.com/watch?v=jdxd_EFDd4s for Angelique's
plea to then prime minister Kevin Rudd to change the law
on assisted suicide.

2 See the discussion of Erin Berg in chapter 14 for more on
the importance of good record keeping.

12 The courage of Caren Jenning

1 See: www.smh.com.au/nsw/state-prosecutors-reasoning-
in-wood-trial-dangerous-20120224-1ttq9.html

2 See: www.theaustralian.com.au/news/nation/queensland-
teacher-jailed-for-helping-suicide-of-man-76/story-e6fr
g6nf-1226272723498

13 Adversaries and allies

1 G. Alcorn, 'Legal or Not, Euthanasia's Controversy Refuses
to Die'. *The Age*, 10 October 1998, p. 1.

2 R. Syme, *A Good Death: An Argument for Voluntary Euthanasia*, Melbourne University Press, 2008, p. 214.

3 F. Stewart, 'Mercy Groups Bicker over Death Pill', *The Sunday Age*, 24 February 2002, p. 4.

4 www.stv.tv/weather/95276-controversial-euthanasia-doctor-speaks-in-glasgow

5 See: www.heraldscotland.com/baby-boomers-are-key-to-winning-euthanasia-debate-says-dr-death-1.826699

6 See: www.ft.com/cms/s/2/60bac5fe-8369-11e1-9f9a-00144feab49a.html#axzz21nOEjb19

7 See, for example: www.bbc.co.uk/news/uk-england-york-north-yorkshire-15588231

8 See: www.bbc.co.uk/news/uk-england-york-north-york shire-15588231

9 www.crikey.com.au/2012/09/17/fight-over-clem-jones-bequest-splits-right-to-die-movement

10 www.exitinternational.net/page/Deliverance

11 www.crikey.com.au/2012/09/17/fight-over-clem-jones-bequest-splits-right-to-die-movement

12 Kathryn Jean Lopez, 'Euthanasia Sets Sail', *National Review Online*, 5 June 2001.

14 My life with the media

1 See, for example: www.theage.com.au/articles/2004/06/08/1086460287472.html

2 L. Scott, 'A Life in Pain Is a Life in Prison', *The Weekend Australian*, 30 March 2002.

3 G. McManus, T. Rindfleisch and I. Haberfield, 'As Crick Debate Rages, a Melbourne Woman Says: I'm Going to End My Life', *Sunday Herald Sun*, 26 May 2002.

4 D. Nason and N. Strahan, 'Nitschke Has Explaining To Do: Premier', *The Australian*, 28 May 2002.

5 The first of Medew's fair reporting in *The Age* on voluntary euthanasia was the quirkily titled '$50 for a Cuppa and

a Recipe to Die' at: www.theage.com.au/news/national
/50-for-a-cuppa-and-recipe-to-die/2008/03/11/12051
25911255.html A second, more serious page-one article
concerned the death of Angie Belecciu and was titled
'Angie's Choice: A Death with Dignity' at: www.theage.
com.au/national/angies-choice-a-death-with-dignity-200
90324-98xs.html

6 www.theage.com.au/national/euthanasia-drug-snares-
younger-australians-20100214-nzgl.html

7 See: www.lifesitenews.com/news/venue-cancels-dr-death-
nitschke-suicide-workshop-in-uk-police-alerted-abou

8 See: www.abc.net.au/radionational/programs/360/losing-
erin/3069486

9 ABC journalist Kirstie Melville would take a similar unbal-
anced line in an episode, 'Losing Erin', of a *Street Stories*
documentary on Radio National at www.abc.net.au/
radionational/programs/360/losing-erin/3069486

10 See: www.abc.net.au/radionational/programs/360/losing-
erin/3069486

11 'Nitschke May Lose Licence Over Beer' at www.ntnews.
com.au/article/2012/09/08/313433_ntnews.html

15 Censorship

1 The full unedited version of *Do It Yourself with Betty* can also
be seen at www.veoh.com/watch/yapi-f4VrKvGKvYw.
Betty's reply to YouTube's censorship can be viewed at
www.peacefulpillhandbook.com/page/MakingtheExitBag

2 www.cbc.ca/fifth/givedeathahand/interview.html

3 See: http://internetphd36.blogspot.com.au/2012/03/fed-
nitschke-says-canadian-suicide-kit.html

4 Read the *Media Watch* transcript at www.abc.net.au/media
watch/transcripts/s1390968.htm

5 The edited segment can be viewed on YouTube under the
title 'Mademoiselle & The Doctor Euthanasia Documentary

Censored Sequence', or tag 'exityourtube', which shows all of Exit's remaining YouTube videos.

6 The transcript can be read at www.abc.net.au/4corners/content/2007/s1916545.htm

6 See: www.smh.com.au/opinion/web-filtering-pulls-plug-on-euthanasia-debate-20090521-bh0s.html

7 Watch the program at www.abc.net.au/4corners/content/2010/s2893505.htm

8 The ad can be viewed at www.youtube.com/watch?v=qRDZFwlWU1s

9 See: www.abc.net.au/news/2010-09-10/pro-euthanasia-tv-ad-banned/2256644

10 See: www.theaustralian.com.au/news/breaking-news/per-cent-support-voluntary-euthanasia-poll/story-fn3dxiwe-1225791455181

11 See: news.smh.com.au/breaking-news-national/another-blow-for-euthanasia-campaign-20100915-15cfd.html

12 The 'Oxford Union' entry in Wikipedia covers the controversy that I experienced at the hands of the Oxford Union.

13 Listen at www.youtube.com/watch?v=QViqeqwj7_E

16 Going global

1 See: www.time.com/time/health/article/0,8599,1890413,00.html

2 On 13 July 2012, the Canadian Government announced it would be appealing the ruling of the BC Supreme Court. This fight is far from over. See: www.sunnewsnetwork.ca/sunnews/politics/archives/2012/07/20120713-142557.html

3 www.sconews.co.uk/news/14380/diy-euthanasia-workshop-allowed-in-edinburgh/

4 See: www.independent.ie/opinion/analysis/dearbhail-mc-donald-courts-facing-tough-task--issue-of-euthanasia-3243698.html

17 Time out

1 To watch the program see www.abc.net.au/tv/messages-tick/video/2008/July2008.htm?pres=s2310447&story=1

2 The group photo of the 1986 trip can be viewed at www.territorystories.nt.gov.au/handle/10070/9342

19 Looking ahead

1 See: legal-dictionary.thefreedictionary.com/Citizen+initiated+referendum

2 See: www.cps.gov.uk/news/press_releases/109_10/

3 See: www.guardian.co.uk/uk/2012/jun/23/tony-nicklinson-assisted-suicide-twitter-interview

4 See: www.bbc.co.uk/news/uk-england-wiltshire-19797634

5 Dennis Shanahan, 'Nitschke Accused of Gas Import Scam', *The Australian*, 31 August 2012, p. 3.

6 Byron Kaye, 'Nitschke Inquiry: AMA Slams AHPRA Inquest', *Medical Observer*, 20 November 2012.

7 Ross Fitzgerald, 'Seriously Ill Should Have the Choice to Exit', *The Australian,* 17 November 2012.

Acknowledgements

Philip Nitschke wishes to thank long-term Exit staff
Kerri Dennis and Amanda McClure.
Peter Corris wishes to thank Jean Bedford and Renee Quinn.

Index